SUPERSTARS

OF THE PREMIER LEAGUE

SUPERSTARS
OF THE PREMIER LEAGUE

·PARRAGON·

Authors: Jim Drewett • Alex Leith Editor: Kevin Whitchurch

A FourFourTwo book

Superstars Of The Premier League

This edition first published by Parragon Book Service Ltd in 1995
Parragon Book Service Ltd
Unit 13-17 Avonbridge Trading Estate
Atlantic Road
Avonmouth
Bristol BS11 9QD
Produced by FourFourTwo, Haymarket Magazines
and Magpie Books Ltd

Cover picture and illustrations courtesy of Empics

Contents

Despite his critics, Tony Adams is a mainstay of Terry Venables' England team.

Tony Adams

Just imagine it. Tony Adams walks out of the tunnel on the first day of the season wearing that famous red number six shirt and salutes the crowd... at the Stretford End. See, you can't, can you? Because Tony Adams is Arsenal right down to those silly hooped socks and an Arsenal team without its long-standing skipper is, frankly, inconceivable.

Former Gunners captain Frank McLintock agrees: 'He's Mr Irreplaceable, it's as simple as that. You don't find many good captains in the game these days, not people like Dave Mackay, Alan Mullery, Tommy Smith and Billy Bremner. But Tony Adams fits that mould. If he ever wanted to leave Arsenal, and I can't believe in his heart of hearts that he ever would, the board should break the bank to keep him. He's a born leader.'

Adams' leadership qualities have never been in doubt, but thanks to the *Daily Mirror*'s graphics department and a few dodgy performances on live TV, the 'donkey' tag's taken a long time to shake off. It's a mark of a man who has had more than his fair share of problems, on and off the pitch, that he's silenced the boo boys and fought his way back into the England set-up.

'Those things that were said about him, the donkey ears and all that, they just served as a stimulant to him,' says Don Howe, who was assistant manager at Arsenal in 1984 when Adams made his debut aged just 17. 'He took it all on the chin and got on with it, just like he always does.'

'Over the years he's had to improve on the ball and he's worked hard at that. But he's a truly great defender. He reads the game superbly, he's a fantastic tackler but he knows exactly when to stand up and jockey as well.'

Adams is a product of an Arsenal youth team which included the likes of Paul Merson, Paul Davis, Michael Thomas and David Rocastle, and Howe recalls: 'It was a real top-notch bunch but Tony was the leader even then.' All but Merson have now fled the Arsenal nest, but Arsenal fans can't bring themselves to imagine that Adams could ever be led astray.

VITAL STATISTICS

Age 28

Date of Birth 10.10.1966

Place of Birth London

League Games & Goals
Arsenal 346[23]

94/95 League sendings-off
1

94/95 League bookings
4

Tony Adams' 94/95 season
It was his testimonial year, he became the Steady Man Of North London (following George's departure), he played just 27 League games, he was inspirational. Just another season for Adams

Honours
Division One champions 1988/89 & 1990/91
FA Cup 1993
Football League Cup 1987 & 1993
European Cup Winners' Cup 1994

Position/Role
Standing tall at the centre of Arsenal's defence, leading exhibitions in synchronized arm raising

Word most often used to describe him
Arsenal

Word never used to describe him
Uncommitted

Arsenal fans pray that
Merson's great talent is
not lost for ever.

Paul Merson was born with outrageous talent. How good a footballer he could have been we'll probably never know, but Arsenal fans have witnessed the prospect of a lifetime transformed into the disappointment of the decade in the space of six short years.

And yet, a brewery-full of lager and a couple of thousand tabloid headlines later, Merson still has the potential to be Arsenal's most creative player. He may have lost that explosive burst of pace but he's still got the balance, he's still got the touch and the eye for a defence-splitting pass that you simply can't teach.

'Paul's a great talent,' says Arsenal legend Frank McLintock. 'I'd just love to be able to see him use it for 90 minutes. I really hope he can come through all his problems because talent like that should never go to waste.'

Merson made his Arsenal debut way back in 1987, aged just 18, though it wasn't until the 1987/88 season that he really started to make an impact, playing 15 games and scoring five times. In Arsenal's championship-winning year the following season, Merson was outstanding.

'A lot of that was due to the role he was playing in the team,' recalls Tim Stevens, editor of the *Arsenal Independent* fanzine. 'He was playing just behind a front line of Niall Quinn, Martin Hayes and Perry Groves and he was getting loads of the ball, loads of knock-downs. He'd kill it, then accelerate, taking on the defence. He had such good balance, he was instinctive, and he scored some spectacular goals as well.'

Stevens reckons Merson was at his peak between 1988 and 1991 but after that he says it was clear from the terraces that Merson had problems.

'It's sad really. He is still a potentially great player but you wonder if he'll ever show it again. During the European Cup Winners' Cup final we were sitting there waiting for him to do something, anything, and it just didn't happen.'

Somewhere inside Paul Merson is an unfair helping of footballing talent, let's hope he starts dishing it out on Premiership defences again this season.

VITAL STATISTICS

Age 27

Date of Birth 20.3.1968

Place of Birth London

League Games & Goals
  Brentford 7[0] loan
  Arsenal 233[62]

94/95 League bookings
  3

Honours
  First Division Championship 1988/89 & 1990/91
  FA Cup 1993
  Coca-Cola Cup 1992
  European Cup Winners' Cup 1994

Transfers
  Loan to Brentford [no fee]

Position/Role
  Playing 'teetotal football' behind the front two

Word most often used to describe him
  Fallen

Word never used to describe him
  Role model

Paul Merson

'He's simply a great player.'
John Hartson.

W

hen Ian Wright decided he wanted a tattoo of something he loved he plumped for a Harley Davidson on his thigh. If he'd waited a couple of months maybe he'd have gone for a picture of John Hartson instead, because until his new strike partner arrived from Luton, Wright was the only player at the club who looked like getting even close to scoring a goal.

Despite having, by his standards, a poor campaign, where would Arsenal be without Wright? Losing away at Barnsley, Port Vale and Huddersfield perchance? After the floodgates failed to open for John Jensen following his first goal for the Gunnners last season, that thingy that happens in the other team's goal that's quite important in football was left, once more, to Wright.

The man signed from Palace for £2 million in 1991, has now scored an incredible 80 goals in 131 League games for Arsenal, and last season he struck 18 of their paltry 52 League goals despite playing in just 30 games. He also fired them almost single-handedly into the European Cup Winners' Cup final.

How familiar that 'Can I Kick It' scene from the Nike ads has become in recent years. Ian Wright slotting the ball hard and low into the Highbury net then celebrating with swaggering hips and salivating tongue. 'Yes you can Ian,' we know.

But if Wright had just been a goal poacher then Arsenal still might have gone down last year. Because with the absence of anything resembling a striking partner for most of the season, he wasn't just finishing his chances. He was creating them as well - witness his 50-yard run through the Aston Villa midfield, defence and Bosnich prior to a more typical Wright finish.

Now that he's playing alongside John Hartson, with his cheeky repertoire of touches and flicks, Arsenal have a strikeforce that *includes* one of the game's most lethal strikers - not just a strikeforce that *is* one of the game's most lethal strikers.

'What can you say about Ian,' says Hartson. 'He's simply a great player. I know I'm going to learn from him and, hopefully, we can create a few chances for each other as well.'

Well it beats relying on John Jensen's finishing.

Ian Wright

VITAL STATISTICS

Age 31

Date of Birth 3.11.1963

Place of Birth Woolwich

League Games & Goals
Crystal Palace 225[90]
Arsenal 131[80]

Honours
Coca-Cola Cup 1993
FA Cup 1993

Transfers
Greenwich Boro to Palace [free]
Palace to Arsenal [£2,500,000]

Position/Role
Scoring goals, snarling & getting booked... all with his collar tucked in

Word used most often to describe him
Booked

Word never used to describe him
Mellow

He's small, he's sharp, he's nippy.
He's hell to play against

Dean Saunders

Dean Saunders cuts in from the left and makes a diagonal run into Tottenham's penalty box, across rather than through a couple of defenders. He waits, waits and then he sees a gap. Blam! He hits the ball on the run and it flies into the net. Another goal, another corker. Deano doesn't seem to like scoring them if they're not crackers.

'He doesn't get many tap-ins,' agrees Allan Evans, Villa stalwart centre-back in the European glory days, now back at the club as assistant manager. 'He's what I call a real striker - he loves to strike the ball from some distance and, if you look at the goals he scores, most of them are pretty spectacular. He's the sort of player I didn't enjoy playing against when I was a defender. He's small, he's sharp, he's nippy. He's hell to play against.'

The 31-year-old Welsh international has plied his glamorous trade across the country from Swansea to Brighton, but the team most people remember him at was the one where he was least happy - Liverpool. Saunders, at £2.9 million the most expensive player at the time in English football, only managed a one-in-four League strike rate for the Reds and was quickly sold on. But he's been much happier in the dimmer limelight at Villa.

'Dean is our top goalscorer again this season and his record speaks for itself... if you look at the goals he's scored over the years you've got to say he's a top-class striker,' continues Evans. 'But you shouldn't just look at goals when you're assessing his importance to the club. Not many people appreciate the amount of work that he does: he's always on the move, buzzing all over the place making runs for his team-mates.'

If anything, Evans reckons Saunders works too hard. 'Our only cause for complaint is that Dean spends too much time in wide positions simply because he's making these runs. He'll be out on the left flank or the right flank when really sometimes you'd prefer him to be in the centre.' Saunders might get more tap-ins from a central position, it's true, but if he did stick in a central role, 'Goal of the Month' just wouldn't be the same.

VITAL STATISTICS

Age 31

Date of Birth 21.6.1964

Place of Birth Swansea

League Games & Goals
Swansea City 49[12]
Cardiff City 3[1]
Brighton 72[20]
Oxford United 59[22]
Derby County 106[42]
Liverpool 42[11]
Aston Villa 73[23]

Honours
FA Cup 1992 [Liverpool]

Transfers
Swansea City to Cardiff City
[loan]
Swansea City to Brighton
[free]
Cardiff City to Oxford Utd
[£60,000]
Oxford Utd to Derby Co
[£1,000,000]
Derby Co to Liverpool
[£2,900,000]
Liverpool to Aston Villa
[£2,300,000]

Position/Role
Here there and everywhere
but always with his tongue
sticking out

**Word most often
used to describe him**
Offside

**Word never used
to describe him**
Scouser

Y

ou could tell that Graeme Souness was starting to lose his grip at Liverpool when he sold full-back Steve Staunton to Aston Villa in 1991 for £1.1 million. In doing so he lost control of the sweetest left foot in the Premier League. With two World Cups under his belt and numerous caps for the Republic of Ireland, the blond bombshell looks a real bargain. And he's still only 26.

'He's all-important to Villa,' says the man who bought him, Ron Atkinson. 'He's a big, big influence especially at corners and free-kicks. He hits a mean dead-ball and many of their goals are directly or indirectly down to him.'

'Nowadays set pieces are hugely important and he's a tremendous asset,' agrees Villa's assistant manager Allan Evans. 'He's a great free-kick taker, it's that left peg of his, he can bend it, he can power it, he can do all sorts of things with it round the box. He also takes corners and with the pace and accuracy he puts on the ball he'll always create problems.'

'His left foot is definitely his biggest asset,' continues Evans. 'He's got the ability to cross the ball in when you wouldn't think it was possible to get a cross in. And that really upsets defenders.'

As a full-back, Staunton makes huge inroads into the opposing half and has proved such a thorn in defenders' sides that nowadays he's as often played in a left-sided midfield role as at left-back. 'He's a good defender, but I like to see him in a position further forward and he'd say the same if you asked him, because he loves to create problems in the opposing defence,' says Evans. 'He can also make accurate passes of 50 to 60 yards which can turn defence to attack very quickly.'

Bargain of the decade? It looks like Liverpool are regretting the day they unloaded the Factor 50 Irishman, plucked from Irish side Dundalk back in 1986. 'I paid just over a million to bring him to Villa,' says Atkinson, 'and considering Liverpool offered £3.5 million to get him back on transfer deadline day last season, you could say it was a good buy.'

This man can make accurate passes of 50 to 60 yards. Blimey.

Steve Staunton

Age 26

Date of Birth 19.1.1969

Place of Birth
Drogheda, Eire

League Games & Goals
Liverpool 55[10]
Bradford City 7[1]
Aston Villa 103[9]

94/95 League bookings
7

Steve Staunton's 94/95 season
Unimpeachable. In a stormy season at Villa Park, he played 34 League games, scored four times (including a point-saver at Norwich) and was Man of the Match on a dozen occasions

Honours
Division 1 Championship 1989/90 [Liverpool]
FA Cup 1989 [Liverpool]

Transfers
Dundalk to Liverpool [£20,000]
Loan to Bradford City [no fee]
Liverpool to Aston Villa [£1,100,000]

Position/Role
Big-hearted, left-footed Irish gem, disguised as freckle-faced Irish schoolboy

Word most often used to describe him
Sickly

Word never used to describe him
Tanned

'He's got what it takes to be a world-class goalkeeper.'
Pat Jennings.

It's the penultimate game of Blackburn's season and they have to win at home to Newcastle. They're 1-0 up but the Geordies are buzzing back at their throats like a swarm of Hitchcockian magpies. Just before half-time Peter Beardsley lets loose a Peter Beardsley screamer from outside the box. It's destined for the top right-hand corner until Tim Flowers somehow, incredibly, hurls himself full stretch to turn it over the bar. Later in the game Gillespie threads through Blackburn's defence and presents Beresford with a certain goal from five yards out. Again Flowers saves. At first it seems the keeper's lucky to be in the right place at the right time, but the 'slomo' replay proves that Flowers has somehow got a hand under his body to stop the ball screaming into the net. Blackburn win the game and go on to grab the title by a hair's breadth. Here's a keeper who wins vital points. Here's a keeper who wins trophies.

'Tim Flowers has got all it takes to make a world-class goalkeeper,' says Pat Jennings, record Northern Ireland cap holder, former Spurs and Arsenal goalie and currently goalkeeping trainer at Tottenham - a man, you could say, who knows a thing or two about life between the sticks. 'He's got agility, he's got good hands, he's got anticipation. He's brave and he reads the game well.'

Flowers, now 28, made his League debut for Wolves way back in 1984 before moving to Southampton two years later. But it's his role in Blackburn's Premiership success last season that has made him the man we might see between England's posts for the next five years or so. 'It's between him and Seaman for the England position, and there's very little to choose between them,' says Jennings. 'But Flowers is so steady. Basically you want the one who'll make the fewest mistakes in goal. Nobody's 100 per cent mistake free, but with Flowers you know he is 99 per cent of the time.'

A keeper's reputation depends on how public and how costly his errors are, as Seaman well knows. And increasingly with Tim Flowers you get the feeling that between opposing strikers' boots and the Blackburn and England net, there lies a pair of hands that will never blunder at the crucial moment. At 28, Tim Flowers is still one for the future.

Tim Flowers

'He's strong, he's determined, he's got a huge future.'
Gary Lineker.

Alan Shearer

W hen Alan Shearer Nat Lofthoused his way through John Beresford's challenge in Blackburn's penultimate game of last season, against Newcastle, heading the ball into the net to put the Lancashire side's title challenge back on the rails, half the country cried 'foul'. Fools.

Shearer was simply doing what he does best: attempting to get a strike in on goal as best he can, using every ounce of strength in his body. And that's some strength. The Geordie-born 24-year-old is a thoroughly modern version of the typical old-fashioned English centre-forward... and has a huge portfolio of swashbuckling goals to prove it.

England's last goalscoring hero, Gary Lineker, has nothing but praise for last season's PFA Player of the Year. 'He's improving all the time,' says Lineker. 'He's strong, he's determined, he's got a terrific shot, he's good in the air. OK, maybe he's not a great dribbler but all round his game is so strong and he knows where he's going.' Shearer actually has the potential to go even further in the game than Lineker did - and England's second top goalscorer admits as much. 'He's got a huge future - he's just got one final step to go, and that's to make it big at international level. He's got to learn new techniques and learn to play new kinds of defenders and systems but I'm sure he'll do it.'

When Shearer first hit the scene in the Southampton youth team his strength was his strength. 'His footwork wasn't the best, it was a bit heavy,' remembers former Saints manager Chris Nicholl. 'I wouldn't say he was naturally gifted. But he was very like Keegan: he worked very hard to improve himself. His sheer determination brought him through.'

Shearer has learned how to make himself a better player. And if he's to threaten Lineker's goal total for England he's going to have to learn a bit more - about the guile of foreign defenders. But learn he will. 'You can learn off everyone and everything,' says Shearer. 'You can learn off watching the TV. If you can't learn then you won't go too far, will you? I'm still learning at 24 and I'm sure I'll be continuing to learn at 34.'

The prospect is frightening.

Age **24**

Date of Birth **13.8.1970**

Place of Birth **Newcastle**

League Games & Goals
Southampton 118[23]
Blackburn 103[81]

94/95 League bookings
4

Alan Shearer's 94/95 season
Played 42 League games, scored 32 times. Now looks rather good value at £3.6 million

Honours
FA Premiership 1994/5

Transfers
Southampton to Blackburn [£3,600,000]

Position/Role
Baggy shorted, old-fashioned swashbuckling centre-forward

Word most often used to describe him
The best

Word never used to describe him
Wasteful

'He always goes out to win.
That's important to us.'
Ray Harford, Blackburn
manager.

didn't have anything to do with the price,' said Chris Sutton after Blackburn broke the British transfer record to sign him from Norwich last summer. 'I never said I was worth £5 million.' But nevertheless opposing fans were looking forward to a few resounding choruses of 'What a waste of money' every time he fluffed a pass or missed the target. Thing is, he rarely did either, wearing the price tag like a pair of wings rather than the lead albatross it could have been. And after a season in which he picked up a championship medal won largely due to his succesful striking partnership with Alan Shearer, he looks worth every penny.

Much of Sutton's success is clearly down to his attitude and temperament, qualities which were under question in the days running up to the big money transfer. Remember the post-nightclub-hiding-in-the-toilets-after-vandalising-a-car shenanigans that hit the headlines in the close season last year? All that's been pushed firmly into the background.

'He's worked very, very hard,' explains Blackburn manager Ray Harford. 'And we like people who work hard here at Blackburn. He's a level-headed young man who's prepared to roll his sleeves up and always go out to win, and that's very important to us.'

Sutton (who started his career as a centre-half) was fortunate that most of the time the spotlight was on Shearer at Blackburn last season, allowing him to settle into the side despite a dodgy start. And, again showing that attitude, he's happy to sit back in the Geordie's shadow. 'I am on a learning curve playing with Alan,' he says. 'He is one of the best strikers in Europe, perhaps in the world, and he simply works hard for the whole team. As far as I am concerned, I am his apprentice.'

With 23 League and Cup goals to his credit last season and a fair share of fantasy football assists to boot, he's got a big future. The £5 million striker is some apprentice, but then again, Shearer's quite a sorcerer.

VITAL STATISTICS

Age **22**

Date of Birth **10.3.1973**

Place of Birth **Nottingham**

League Games & Goals
Norwich 102[35]
Blackburn 40[15]

94/95 League bookings
7

Honours
Premiership 1994/5

Transfers
Norwich to Blackburn
[£5,000,000]

Position/Role
Following his big buddy Shearer around, feeding off his leftovers

Word most often used to describe him
Copycat

Word never used to describe him
Lone striker

Chris Sutton

The Eire international now gets his chance in the Premiership.

I f Bolton hadn't made the Premiership then chances are you wouldn't have seen Jason McAteer at Burnden Park for dust. Now it looks like Wanderers might hang on to their Republic of Ireland star and the dust he'll be kicking up come August will be into the faces of the big boys of the top flight.

A World Cup veteran at 24, the Premiership is not where McAteer thinks he belongs, he knows it. 'He's a typical scouser, bubbly, cheeky and brimming over with confidence,' says *Bolton Evening News* sports editor Peter Mensworth. 'He's got the world at his feet now. I only hope he can keep those feet on the ground - hopefully at Bolton.'

McAteer, who started his career at Northern Premier League Marine but was picked for the first team only twice, was converted from a right-sided midfielder to a 'box to box' central midfielder by Bolton boss Bruce Rioch when he arrived at Burnden Park in 1992.

'He's at his best charging from one end of the pitch to the other,' says Mensworth. 'But he's got pace and touch to go with his lung-busting runs.'

When he's with Ireland, however, Jack Charlton plays McAteer on the right side and there are many in the game who believe that's where he's most effective. With David Lee hogging the touchline at Bolton, Rioch had to create another role for his young star but in the long run he may well end up on the flank - be it for Bolton or, many believe one day soon, his home-town club Liverpool.

The only criticism you'll hear in Bolton of the nifty-footed pin-up boy of north Lancashire is that he doesn't score enough goals. Eight in 108 league games is not the sort of return expected of a thrusting midfielder but Rioch believes that side of his game will come with 'more experience in the killing zone'.

World Cups, cup runs, Wembley finals and promotion pushes, it's been a fairytale three years for Jason McAteer. And you get the feeling that whatever happens to Bolton Wanderers in the Premiership, there's always going to be a happy ending for him.

Jason McAteer

VITAL STATISTICS

Age 24

Date of Birth 18.6.1971

Place of Birth Liverpool

League Games & Goals
Bolton Wanderers 108[8]

94/95 League bookings
4

Jason McAteer's 94/95 season
Disappointed at Wembley in the Coca-Cola final, lucky to stay on in the play-off final. Played 43 League games (phew), scoring five times. Man of the Match 12 times

Transfers
Marine to Bolton [unknown]

Position/Role
Running up and down like a nutter, showing off how young, fit and skilful he is

Word most often used to describe him
Magnificent

Word(s) never used to describe him
Quite good

From Sampdoria to
Stamford Bridge;
Gullit teams up
with Hoddle.

When Ruud Gullit was a whippersnapper 17-year-old with in-yer-face dreadlocks playing for Haarlem in Holland in 1980 two men went a-scouting to look at him: Don Howe, then of Arsenal, and Ipswich's Bobby Robson. Although the asking price was a mere £80,000, neither man thought him good enough to bring to England. Gullit turned into one of the best attackers of the game, won everything worth winning with club and country (give or take the odd World Cup) and, in the twilight of his career, has ended up earning that sort of money every fortnight with a lucrative deal... at Chelsea.

The funny thing is that Gullit wasn't playing upfront back in those days, he was playing as a sweeper, and it was Glenn Hoddle's willingness to let him play in his old position (as well as a sackful of dosh) that made Gullit decide to move to the Bridge. 'Chelsea have offered me the opportunity of a new challenge after eight years in Italy where I won everything I wanted to,' he said on signing. 'Now I look forward to coming to England to play here.'

It's a sign of the health of English soccer (despite the violence, despite the sleaze) that Gullit is taking over where Klinsmann left off, and his arrival in south-west London has caused an unprecedented flurry in the Chelsea season-ticket office. 'Gullit will fill Stamford Bridge every week and add 10,000 at every other stadium,' says Ruud's former Samp team-mate, England captain David Platt.

Sceptics will point to the Amsterdammer's age, but Platt doesn't reckon that'll diminish Gullit's performances. 'He has looked after himself and I'll sure he'll make an impact in English football. Age doesn't come into it if you are in good physical condition.'

Gullit, a socialist who dedicated his European Footballer of the Year award to the then-behind-bars Nelson Mandela, is one of the most charismatic players in the world and his signing has started up a wave of Gullitmania in the capital. Expect to see a few wacky wigs in the crowd at Stamford Bridge this season.

VITAL STATISTICS

Age 32

Date of Birth 1.9.1962

Place of Birth Amsterdam

League Games & Goals
  Haarlem 91[32]
  Feyenoord 85[40]
  PSV 68[46]
  Milan 125[38]
  Sampdoria 31[15]

Honours
  European Championship
  (Holland) 1988
  Italian Scudetto (Milan)
  1988, 1992,1993
  European Cup (Milan)
  1989, 1990

Position/Role
  Mr nice guy European
  football ambassador cum
  striker/sweeper
  extraordinaire

**Word most often
used to describe him**
  Dreadlocked

**Word never used
to describe him**
  Average

RuudGullit

'I'd like to see a little more aggression from him.' Ron Atkinson, Coventry City manager.

Dion Dublin, what a nice guy. Too nice, though, according to his manager Ron Atkinson who wants to see a bit less smiling and a lot more snarling from his skipper.

'Dion's a great player with a nice disposition, but maybe that's something that's got to change if he's to make an even bigger impact on the game,' says Atkinson. 'If you look at most top strikers you'll see fire in their eyes, and I'd like to see a little more of that from Dion, a little more aggression.'

It's not that Atkinson's displeased, it's just that having worked with the former Cambridge and Manchester United hit-man first hand he feels he can get even better. 'He's obviously benefited from playing alongside the likes of Hughes and Cantona at United,' continues Atkinson. 'But I believe he can keep on improving.' A £1 million buy from Cambridge in August 1992, a few eyebrows were raised when Phil Neal gambled nearly twice that amount one broken leg, just 12 league outings and two goals later. In his second game Neal made the Marvin Hagler lookalike captain of the struggling Midlanders (more raised eyebrows) and entrusted him with restoring Sky Blue fortunes. Dublin responded with ten goals in 13 games (including a debut strike at QPR and an audacious overhead kick at Everton), plenty of talking on the pitch and a desire to win often masked by that big white grin that Atkinson wants to see less of.

It's all a long way from playing centre-half for Cambridge reserves, but that's where Dublin ended up after nine games and five goals for Norwich reserves (it's not like Norwich to let go of a good striker). His break came wearing the number nine shirt for John Beck's 'up and under' Cambridge side and he soon found himself the focus of everything the other ten players could throw at him. The rest is history.

Now he's playing and scoring regularly in an increasingly stylish Atkinson- and Strachan-inspired Coventry side and Dublin's ability in the air is being recognised as just one, albeit major, facet of his game. Witness the Sky Blues' final goal in the 3-1 victory against Tottenham at the end of last season, an exquisite move clinically finished by Dublin with a neat half-volley - the kind of goal some thought he could never score.

VITAL STATISTICS

Age 26

Date of Birth 22.4.1969

Place of Birth Leicester

League Games & Goals
Cambridge United 156[52]
Manchester United 12[2]
Coventry 31[13]

Honours
1990/91 Division 3 title
[Cambridge Utd]

Transfers
Norwich to Cambridge Utd
[free]
Cambridge Utd to Man Utd
[£1,000,000]
Man Utd to Coventry
[£2,100,000]

Position/Role
Smiling down at
flustered centre-halves

**Word most often
used to describe him**
Handful

**Word never used
to describe him**
Miserable

Dion Dublin

'He scored more than 20 goals for us last season and he was injured for half of it.'
Ron Atkinson, Coventry City manager.

You can only just get a half-decent car for £10,000 these days, but in 1991 you could get a high speed, low mileage Peter Ndlovu. Ten grand for a man who, when he's on song, doesn't just tear defences apart but slices them to shreds before they've even had a chance to move.

Coventry's African jewel, still only 22, is a huge hero back home in his native Zimbabwe and has his fair share of Premiership admirers outside Highfield Road too (Kenny Dalglish and Kevin Keegan in particular), yet so far Coventry have managed to hang on to their most valuable asset - and manager Ron Atkinson isn't complaining.

'He's a quality, quality player,' says Atkinson. 'He's got a few tricks in his locker, sure, but the best one of all is being able to beat the last man and score. And he's getting better and better at that all the time.'

'We're still trying to work out whether his best position is down the middle or on the wing, but he still scored more than 20 goals for us last season and he was injured for half of it.'

In a league which is still strangely cautious of signing African players (look how many are playing in the French, Belgian, Dutch and German leagues), Ndlovu has shown breathtaking ball-at-his-feet skill, frightening pace and lethal finishing even in cold weather (did you see his Coca-Cola Cup goal at West Brom, Ron Noades?).

The Zimbabwean international - who made his debut aged just 19 - has been at Coventry three-and-a-half years now. Maybe he'll stay and blossom yet further under the wily guidance of Ron Atkinson and Gordon Strachan. 'I'm the kind of person who takes advice well. I'll listen to anybody because you can always learn more things about the game and about yourself,' he says.

And, contrary to his natural instincts, Ndlovu says he's in no hurry to go anywhere. 'I'm very proud of Coventry City, they gave me a chance to play here and I love playing for them.'

Peter Ndlovu

Age **22**

Date of Birth **25.2.1973**

Place of Birth **Zimbabwe**

League Games & Goals
Coventry 125[31]

94/95 League bookings
0

Peter Ndlovu's 94/95 season
Played in 30 League games, scoring 11 times, including that cracker that had Man United rocking in April

Transfers
Highlanders to Coventry [£10.000]

Position/Role
A yard in front of where the laws of time and motion say he should be

Word(s) most often used to describe him
'What was that'

Word never used to describe him
Sluggish

Duncan Ferguson

'The most frightening player I've seen in the Premiership for a long time.' Duncan MacKenzie.

Duncan Ferguson is the best Everton striker since Alex Young. He's good looking, articulate, looks after his mum, loves animals and does a lot of work for charity. Okay call me chicken, but would you say anything different about the man they call 'Duncan Disorderly' and whose assaults, shall we say, haven't always been directed towards the opposition's goal?

When Ferguson turned up on loan at Goodison Park last season with a hard-man reputation and a string of suspended sentences and bans, no-one knew quite what to expect. When he scored in the 2-0 victory over Liverpool, no-one on the blue side of Merseyside cared, and when it later turned out he'd spent the night before out on the town - including getting arrested for drink driving - his cult status was secured.

'Big Fergie likes a few pints, loves to stay out late and chase the birds, and give a bit of lip in training,' observed legendary Scottish striker, drinker and womaniser, Jim Baxter. 'In my book he's got all the perfect ingredients of a great footballer.'

One £4.3 million transfer, six goals and an FA Cup winner's medal later, the towering young Scot, still only 23, has all but proved the theory. Quick with his feet but truly awesome in the air, last season Ferguson channelled all that natural aggression into keeping the Toffees in the Premiership, terrifying the life out of a few defenders along the way.

'He's the most frightening player I've seen in the Premiership for a long time,' said ex-Everton forward Duncan MacKenzie, and former Raith Rovers full-back John McStay probably agrees. It was Ferguson's 'disagreement' with McStay's forehead during his turbulent 'few appearances, few goals' spell at Glasgow Rangers (following a then British record £4 million move from Dundee Utd in 1993) that's likely to see the Everton wild man spending some of the season in the stands - if not behind bars - thanks to a 12-match suspended ban imposed by the Scottish FA.

But although it may be a while before he's unleashed on Premiership defences again, when he does reappear in the Royle blue of Everton, one thing's for certain - he'll be back with a bang.

VITAL STATISTICS

Age 23

Date of Birth 27.12.1971

Place of Birth Stirling

League Games & Goals
Dundee United 77[28]
Rangers 10[1]
Everton 23[6]

94/95 League sendings-off
2

94/95 League bookings
1

Duncan Ferguson's 94/95 season
Played 23 times in the League, scoring seven times. Undid many Premiership defences with his uncompromising approach

Honours
FA Cup 1995

Position/Role
A foot higher in the air than most wimpy English defenders

Word most often used to describe him
Sir

Word never used to describe him
Sweet

Our Nev, a genuine
Merseyside hero.

Neville

He does what he likes and says what he thinks. He drinks nothing stronger than tea and yes, he used to be a dustman. He's Neville Southall, Everton's very own Welsh mountain, and he does things his way.

'Neville is different,' admits Toffees manager Joe Royle. 'But as a goalkeeper he's in a different class.'

For 15 solid years Southall has stood granite-like between the sticks at Goodison Park. He's won championships, FA Cups, European trophies and Player of the Year awards. He's staged an on the pitch sit-in (at half-time when 3-0 down v Leeds in 1985), refused to wear flourescent goalkeepers' tops (insisting Umbro provide him with black or grey) and he even skipped the recent FA Cup-winning celebrations to get back to his home in Llandudno, the town on the Welsh coast where he was born.

In fact it's hard to imagine Everton without Southall in goal, but when Joe Royle arrived the word was that it seemed to spell the end of the road for Wales' most capped player (80 caps). One FA Cup final and a successful fight for Premiership survival later and it is a different story, though with Southall you never quite know what to expect next.

'Since I came he has not cost us a single goal,' enthuses Royle. And Southall says he's warmed to the man he feared would arrive wielding an axe. Typically, the big keeper refuses to be drawn on his future with the club he joined as a 21 year old from Bury (where he'd played just 39 games) for £150,000 back in 1981.

Decidedly un-flash - he cycled to training until finally learning to drive in his mid-twenties - Southall knows he's only got a season or two left at the very top. But while he's in the kind of dominating, safe handling, body-filling-the-entire-goal kind of form he showed at the end of last season, Joe Royle knows that if he wants him he can rely on Southall for a few more big games yet - if 'Big Nev' decides he wants to stick around, that is.

VITAL STATISTICS

Age 38

Date of Birth 16.9.1958

Place of Birth Llandudno

League Games & Goals
Bury 39
Port Vale 9 loan
Everton 494

Honours
Division One 1985 & 1987
FA Cup 1984 & 1994
European Cup Winners' Cup 1985

Transfers
Bangor City then Winsford Utd [fees not recorded/relevant]
Winsford to Bury [£6,000]
Bury to Everton [£150,000]
Port Vale [loan]

Position/Role
Standing Mount Snowdon-like in Everton's goal

Word most often used to describe him
Legend

Word never used to describe him
Sheepish

Southall

Gary McAllister,
short of hair but not
short of options

Garʏ

t's the first minute of the Rangers v Leeds European Cup tie at Ibrox in 1992. A Leeds cross is headed out to the edge of the box. It falls to the wrong man. One of Gary McAllister's trademarks is a crisp, rasping volley and before you can say 'Hot Shot Hamish', the ball is spinning into the Rangers net. A dream start for Leeds, but eventually it's not enough to see them through. They haven't played in Europe since.

Until now that is. McAllister is now Leeds captain (as well as skipper of Scotland) and under him the team made a late surge to catch up with lead-booted Newcastle and earn a place in the UEFA Cup. 'We were pleased with the way the end of the season went, especially as we finished the form side and were looking better than both Manchester United and Blackburn. And we could improve on that position next season,' he says.

McAllister was the driving force behind Leeds' late run, with his cool head and astute don't-waste-possession passing. 'I felt I had a pretty good season: I was consistent,' he says, 'partially because I played every match but one.'

McAllister's midfield style - simple ball, simple ball, outrageous spot-on 50-yard pass - is reminiscent of Glenn Hoddle so it's no surprise the Chelsea manager was an early role model for Gary. 'The players I most modelled myself on were Ray Wilkins and particularly Glenn Hoddle. I admired Hoddle's technique, his touch, his ability to control the ball and always pick the right pass, whether it was long or short. He'd always put his head up to look at his options and I'd like to think I've learnt that lesson off him,' he says.

Hoddle and Wilkins, of course, both played in Europe, and McAllister, who Leeds bought from Leicester for £1.2m in 1991, is looking forward to Leeds' return to continental competition. 'I'll particularly enjoy playing in Europe because the game tends to be a bit slower, which gives you more time on the ball, more time to work out your options.' In the frenetic cut-and-thrust of the Premiership McAllister rarely looks short of space, or short of options. UEFA Cup opponents beware.

Age 30

Date of Birth 25.12.1964

Place of Birth
Motherwell

League Games & Goals
Motherwell 59[6]
Leicester 201[46]
Leeds 195[27]

Honours
First Division Championship 1991/92

Transfers
Motherwell to Leicester [£125,000]
Leicester to Leeds [£1,000,000]

Position/Role
Chilling out in the middle of the park while everyone else gets frantic

Word most often used to describe him
Composed

Word never used to describe him
Reckless

McAllister

ast season, Leeds' campaign looked to be over in February. Out of the Coca-Cola Cup, drawn against Man United in the FA Cup, just above mid-table in the Premiership - Howard Wilkinson's side had been blowing hot and cold all season. And then along came Tony Yeboah.

The Ghanaian international was top scorer in the Bundesliga at the time but fell out with Eintracht Frankfurt manager Jupp Heynkes over training routines and wanted out. He eventually signed for £3.4 million, which now seems a snip in these days of £7 million Andy Coles and £8.5 million Stan Collymores.

'The arrival of Tony Yeboah has helped us so much because his finishing in the box is so lethal,' says Gary Speed on 'Yebbo's' role in the Leeds revival. 'That gives the rest of us a real boost. He's so cool and confident and that's contributed so much to our good form this year.'

Skipper Gary McAllister is equally complimentary. 'He's an out and out goalscorer. But it's the way he puts the ball in the net that's interesting. I don't think he blasted one in all season. He lets the keeper make the first move, and then lifts it over him or slots it past him. He passes it into the goal.'

What strikes you about Yeboah, who is known as the 'goal king' in Ghana, is his incredible confidence. Take the winner he scored against Newcastle in the crucial late season UEFA dogfight. One on one with Pavel Srnicek, he rounded the keeper, celebrated the goal, and then put it in the net.

'My role model when I was growing up was Pele,' says Yeboah. 'He was probably the world's best ever player. Now I look up to Romario because he is both a good goalscorer and an excellent dribbler.'

With the cool head of one and the arrogance of the other, with as many goals for Leeds in a third of a season as Brian Deane has scored in two years, Leeds are delighted to have hung onto Yeboah for another season. Premiership defenders are rather less impressed.

'He just passes it into the goal.'
Gary McAllister, Leeds captain.

Tony Yeboah

VITAL STATISTICS

Age **28**

Date of Birth **6.6.1966**

Place of Birth **Ghana**

League Games & Goals
**Eintracht Frankfurt 109[61]
Leeds 18[13]**

94/95 League bookings
0

Tony Yeboah's 94/95 season
Played in 18 League games, scored 12 times including a first-half hat-trick against Ipswich and the only goal of the match in his debut against Everton

Position/Role
Goal-poaching puma

Word most often used to describe him
Deadly

Word never used to describe him
Pussy-footed

The man with the £8.5 million price tag.

Sta

With his Yaz-lookalike haircut, 'the only way is up' for Stan Collymore. Despite his worryingly frequent accidents with the peroxide bottle, the striker who just seems to get better and better (he scored 18 goals in 28 games for Forest last season) was far and away the most sought-after striker in the Premiership this summer.

Ian Edwards, Forest correspondent for the *Nottingham Evening Post*, believes the new Liverpool man has the potential to become the best England striker for years.

'Stan's got everything,' he explains. 'He's got pace, he's good in the air, he can turn, he's good with his head. At the moment Shearer is a better all-round player but I'm certain Stan could be even better.'

Unfortunately for Forest it all went sour last season. The star striker criticised his team-mates for not giving him the right service, had a mid-season bust up with manager Frank Clark and then declared his future lay elsewhere after learning of Villa's bid for him via the press and not the club.

'The trouble with Stan is that if everything isn't hunky-dory then it's everyone else's fault,' says Edwards. 'He really needs to mature a bit and sort his attitude out. Last season he was so up and down, when he was on song he was out of this world but when he wasn't up for it, well he wasn't up for it. You'd be able to tell in the first five minutes, just by his first touch or so, what sort of a game he was going to have.'

Collymore started his career at Stafford Rangers, signing for Crystal Palace when he was 19 but apparently unable to handle the Wright- and Bright-inspired training ground banter. So Palace sold the boy with the Brummie accent to Southend for £150,000 and Barry Fry brought the best out of him. Thirty games and 15 goals later he was on his way to newly relegated Forest for £2.2 million, though if Brian Clough hadn't stalled over cash the previous season maybe he'd have been lining up in the Premiership a year earlier. Now his two-season Forest chapter is over, and Stan the Man is heading to Anfield. Although there's no doubt he's good, the £8.5 million price tag demands greatness. Merseyside, and the football world, is watching closely.

VITAL STATISTICS

Age 24

Date of Birth 22.1.1971

Place of Birth Stone

League Games & Goals
Crystal Palace 20[1]
Southend 30[15]
Nottingham Forest 64[40]

Transfers
Wolves to Stafford Rangers [no fee recorded]
Stafford to Palace [£100,000]
Palace to Southend [£100,000]
Southend to Nottm Forest [£2,000,000]
Nottm Forest 10to Liverpool [£8,500,000]

Position/Role
Going for goal but not giving a monkeys what he looks like

Word most often used to describe him
Yaz-like

Word never used to describe him
Settled

Collymore

Robbie Fowler's strengths? 'He scores goals.' Ronnie Moran, Liverpool coach.

What are Robbie Fowler's strengths? OK it's a stupid question but Ronnie Moran's reply isn't. 'He scores goals,' says the Liverpool coach.

Banging in 25 goals in 42 League games and winning the PFA Young Player of the Year award would be enough to make anyone run around with their shirt on back to front, but the 21-year-old Liverpool hot shot who did just that in 1994/95 is just about managing to keep his feet on the ground.

'You've got to have a certain arrogance to be a good player, but Robbie's no big-head,' says Moran. 'There's so much going on in the heads of these young players, especially if they become superstars, and some can handle it and some can't. Robbie can.'

In fact Fowler's desire to avoid the glare of publicity off the pitch is well publicised. He lets his feet do the talking and his record since scoring on his Liverpool debut in the Coca-Cola Cup against Fulham two years ago is astounding. Thirty seven League goals in 70 games is some record.

But it was in the white shirt of England not the red shirt of Liverpool that Fowler made his name for himself. The 1993 European Youth Championships saw Fowler come off the bench in the first game against France and proceed to fire England to victory in the tournament with five goals in five games, including a stunning hat-trick against Spain.

England youth-team manager Ted Powell remembers it well. 'Robbie was outstanding. His finishing was lethal, with both feet, and it's great to see him doing so well at Liverpool. He had a great attitude, he was always ready to listen and learn, and I'm sure his success then has helped him get where he is now.'

But Ronnie Moran has a warning for his young star. 'Robbie's got to put last season behind him now. It wouldn't matter if he scored 60 goals last year, he's got to start all over again. Like every player here, he's got to prove himself in every game he plays in.'

Sounds like Premiership defences are in for a pretty hard time of it again this season.

VITAL STATISTICS

Age 20

Date of Birth 9.4.1975

Place of Birth Liverpool

League Games & Goals
   Liverpool 70[37]

94/95 League bookings
   4

Robbie Fowler's 94/95 season
   Played in 41 League games, scoring 25 times. He was the scourge of Arsenal, scoring a hat-trick at Anfield and a last-minute winner at Highbury

Honours
   Coca-Cola Cup 1995

Position/Role
   Nipping in front of Ian Rush to score again

Word most often used to describe him
   Clinical

Word never used to describe him
   Erratic

Robbie Fowler

When asked recently what he'd like to have with him if he happened to be marooned on a desert island, Steve McManaman replied: 'Pele, so he could teach me a few things.' The way the young Liverpool midfielder played last season, however, the world's greatest ever footballer might find the lessons equally rewarding.

McManaman's breathtaking ability to run at and beat defenders at will, his spindly body gyrating wildly and the ball apparently glued to his left foot, inevitably smacks of the days when shorts were baggy (yes, even baggier than Blackburn's current design) and every team had two wingers. He stirred a few fond memories last season, not least in the wing wizard himself Sir Stanley Matthews who complimented him on his 'dribbling' before he went out and single-handedly demolished Bolton in the Coca-Cola Cup final.

But McManaman is not really a winger. His strength is not beating men, getting to the by-line and firing in crosses, he's at his best when he's skipping past tackles and going straight for goal.

'I was given a free role last season and it allowed me to get forward pretty well as much as I like,' he says. 'I was just going out there and running at defenders. It was great, but the whole team was playing well which made it much easier.'

McManaman is clearly very much in Terry Venables' England thoughts and, for the first time in his three-year first-team career, his club place looks secure. He's now played more than 120 League games for Liverpool after being snapped up from right under the noses of the Everton scouts as an 11 year old - ironic seeing that he was a true blue Everton fan with Bob Latchford and Duncan MacKenzie posters plastered all over his walls.

'He always had confidence, even then,' recalls Liverpool coach Ronnie Moran. 'When you saw him coming down the corridor you'd think: "Aye, aye, who's this then." He walked with a swagger like he does now. But he's no big-head, he's a sensible lad who looks after himself, and that's why he's made it.'

The wing wizard himself, Sir Stanley Matthews, has complimented McManaman on his 'dribbling'.

Steve McManam

VITAL STATISTICS

Age 23

Date of Birth 11.2.1972

Place of Birth Liverpool

League Games & Goals
Liverpool 144[19]

94/95 League bookings
5

Steve McManaman's 94/95 season
Played in 40 League games, scored 7 goals but made a lot more. Team-mates Fowler (25 goals) and Rush (12) thrived on his service

Honours
1992 FA Cup
1995 Coca-Cola Cup

Position/Role
Roaming around making defenders look stupid

Word most often used to describe him
Scally

Word never used to describe him
Solid

Unflappable,
quick-thinking,
slick-passing
Jamie Redknapp.

Jami

The only thing that went wrong for Jamie Redknapp last year was that Ryan Giggs stole his girlfriend.

Apart from that one romantic hiccup, he starred in a Liverpool team that increasingly resembles the Anfield sides of old, winning a Coca-Cola Cup winner's medal in the process and receiving his first call-up into the full England squad for the match against Uruguay in February.

Suddenly the baby-faced captain of England's Under-21 side is starting to fulfil the potential that half of football - not just his West Ham manager dad Harry - has known about for years.

Terry Venables nurtured his silky schoolboy skills when he was manager at Spurs and coveted his signature - until Jamie went to join Dad down at Bournemouth and then, ouch, signed for Liverpool for £350,000 in 1990.

After three years growing up and finding his feet at Anfield, Redknapp has emerged as the unflappable, quick-thinking, slick-passing base for Liverpool's fight back to the top. 'It's great playing with Jamie,' jokes Steve McManaman. 'He does all the running and I just get to go forward.'

Dave Sexton, manager of England's Under-21 side, speaks of Redknapp in glowing terms. 'His biggest asset is his confidence on the ball,' says Sexton. 'He's always looking to accept it, no matter what the circumstances, and he rarely gives it away once he's got it.'

'By instinct he's a midfield general,' continues Sexton, 'but I think my only criticism of him is that he should score more goals.' He's scored just 10 times for the Reds in four seasons although he has notched five in 18 Under-21 appearances. 'He should be looking to make more runs into the box,' says Sexton. 'But that will come. He's a confident, enthusiastic, good-natured boy who loves the game and wants so much to get on and do well - which he definitely will.'

This season Jamie's got to mix a little more flair and a little more of the unexpected to his consistently smooth blend of midfield mastery. If he does that then he's got all the ingredients to make a future England player and Liverpool might just have a recipe for Premiership success.

Age 22

Date of Birth 25.6.1973

Place of Birth
Barton on Sea

League Games & Goals
Bournemouth 13
Liverpool 97[10]

94/95 League bookings
5

Honours
Coca-Cola Cup 1995

Transfers
Bournemouth to Liverpool
[£350,000]

Position/Role
Calmly stroking the ball around Liverpool's clustered midfield with glowing cheeks

Word most often used to describe him
Smoothie

Word never used to describe him
Unshaven

Redknapp

'The quickest there is.
He could catch pigeons.'
    bby Gould,
    mbledon manager.

Keith Curle

hen Sam Hammam first saw Keith Curle play he described him as 'the Rolls Royce of pace'.

Hammam and the Wimbledon manager Bobby Gould had just seen Curle play for Reading. Gould was about to persuade his chairman to part with £500,000 for the classy centre-back and told him: 'I'll triple your money in three years.' And he did.

'I wanted to create the fastest back four in Europe,' recalls Gould. 'And Curle is the quickest there is. I had him as lad at Bristol Rovers and he could catch pigeons - but he was playing in midfield and he couldn't cross the ball. It was Terry Cooper at Bristol City who saw his potential as a defender and, after moving from full-back to centre-back, he went from strength to strength.'

After two-and-a-half seasons with the Dons, forming a solid partnership in the middle with future £3 million man John Scales, Curle moved on to Peter Reid's Manchester City for £2 million.

He was picked for Graham Taylor's doomed 1992 European Championship squad and played (at right-back) in the disastrous early games in Sweden.

It was all a long way from Elm Park, Reading, but that's where Curle had moved to from Bristol City in 1987 as a rejuvenated centre-half, despite attracting the attention of bigger clubs. After two years at Reading - taking part in a sensational Simod Cup victory (if there is such a thing) over Luton in 1988 - he chose to link up with Gould at Wimbledon before signing for City.

At Maine Road he's been made skipper, seen two managers shown the door and, like the club, has struggled at times to find the form that should be second nature.

Nevertheless he's a classy defender and his ability to get in a last-ditch tackle as well as his ice-cool penalty-taking technique and post spot-kick celebrations have made him a firm favourite with the Maine Road faithful.

How, just like those fans, he must dream of a consistently strong Manchester City side pushing for honours - you get the feeling that a truly great defender might emerge if that were to happen.

Age 31

Date of Birth 14.11.1963

Place of Birth Bristol

League Games & Goals
Bristol Rovers 32[4]
Torquay United 18[5]
Bristol City 121[1]
Reading 40[0]
Wimbledon 93[3]
Manchester City 108[8]

Honours
Simod Cup 1988 [Read.

Transfers
**Bristol Rovers to Torquay
[£5,000]**
**Torquay to Bristol City
[£10,000]**
**Bristol City to Reading
[£150,000]**
**Reading to Wimbledon
[£500,000]**
**Wimbledon to Man City
[£2,500,000]**

Position/Role
**Getting in front of defenders
even if they've had seven
minutes head start and a
bottle of Lucozade before
the match**

Word most often
used to describe him
Supersonic

Word never used
to describe him
Slowcoach

'I love the type of football played here in England.'
Uwe Rosler.

Jurgen Klinsmann's departure was the big news at the end of last season, but that still leaves one German striker in the Premiership and he's planning to make a few headlines himself this time.

Uwe Rosler arrived at Maine Road from Dynamo Dresden at the end of the 1993/94 season and battled his way into City fans' hearts with five crucial, Premiership-status-ensuring goals. And in his first full season at the club last time out he showed a consistent goalscoring touch, notching 22 in 36 starts - a pretty good tally in any team, let alone one struggling for points.

'I love the type of football played here in England,' says Rosler. 'It's physical, it's fast and it's very good for strikers because you get so many chances.' He likes it so much, in fact, that, unlike Klinnsman, he is planning to stick around for a while. 'In Germany there is another style of football I don't so much like, so I see my future here in England,' he insists.

Rosler's let's-get-the-ball-in-the-net way of leading the line has been aided by the way sacked manager Brian 'Nobby' Horton had the Blues playing last season. 'We have a very good offensive side here at City,' enthuses Rosler. 'And I must say thank you very much to Peter Beagrie, Nicky Summerbee and Paul Walsh for giving me a lot of assists for my goals. This is a good team and it must stay together, especially the 4-4-2 formation with two wingers that provided me with so many crosses.'

Another season, another manager, however, and it remains to be seen what sort of tactics we'll see at Maine Road this season. One thing's for sure though. Rosler's been in such hot form that only a fool or a zealous Eurosceptic would leave the Leipzig-born striker out of this season's side, especially as an international career beckons; Rosler cites Rudi Voeller as a major role model, and with the latter's international career at an end, German manager Berti Vogts is taking a close look at our Uwe as a possible replacement.

Age 27

Date of Birth 15.11.1968

Place of Birth Attenburg, East Germany

League Games & Goals
Manchester City 48[27]

94/95 League sendings-off
1

94/95 League bookings
6

Uwe Rosler's 94/95 season
Played 31 League games, scored 14 times. Man of the Match six times. City's lifesaver

Transfers
Dynamo Dresden to Man City [£750,000]

Position/Role
Goalsniffing rottweiller in the centre of the attack

Word most often used to describe him
Lethal

Word never used to describe him (yet)
Leaving

Uwe Rosler

'Cantona is arrogant, a bad loser and believes people should give him more respect'.
Richard Kurt, editor, *United We Stood*.

Eric Cantona

Arrogant, paranoid and outrageously talented. It's funny how a breakdown of Eric Cantona's personality sounds like a pretty good character analaysis of Manchester United football club. 'Cantona encapsulates everything that we love about Manchester United,' says Richard Kurt, editor of Man U fanzine *United We Stood*. 'Cantona is arrogant, he's a bad loser, he believes people should give him more respect - that's our club, that's us, and apart from his appeal in footballing terms, which is obvious, that's why he is so adored.'

That adoration, it appears, is mutual. For when his ban is completed and the kids of Manchester have been converted from spotty herberts to maverick geniuses in just 100 or so hours of community service, against all the odds Cantona will again pull on that famous number seven shirt.

'At United the individual is everything,' says Kurt. 'It's not like Liverpool, where the humble stars are cogs in a greater machine. United sides are traditionally collections of individuals rather than teams, and Cantona is the ultimate individual. He's different just like United are different.'

Of course none of this would carry any weight if Cantona wasn't a half decent player. But when the inspirational Frenchman arrived at United from Leeds in that sensational £1.2 million deal in 1992, the Reds hadn't scored for four games and yet another title challenge looked to be going down the tube. Twenty two genius-packed games and nine goals later the trophy was in the bag and United were on a three-year roll... a roll which ended only when Matthew Simmons went and mentioned Eric's mother.

United and Cantona are now synoynymous. He loves the club, the club (and especially the fans) love him. But no wonder. In the last two seasons he's scored 38 goals for his club and made another 25. He can score goals from inside or outside the area, with either foot, or his head, from open play or from set pieces. He is, not to beat about the bush, the best player in the Premier League. His boss, Alex Ferguson, calls him 'the best I've ever worked with'. For a manager who's worked with Gordon Strachan and Bryan Robson that's no small praise. When he returns Cantona will have a heightened sense of injustice and six months' rest behind him.

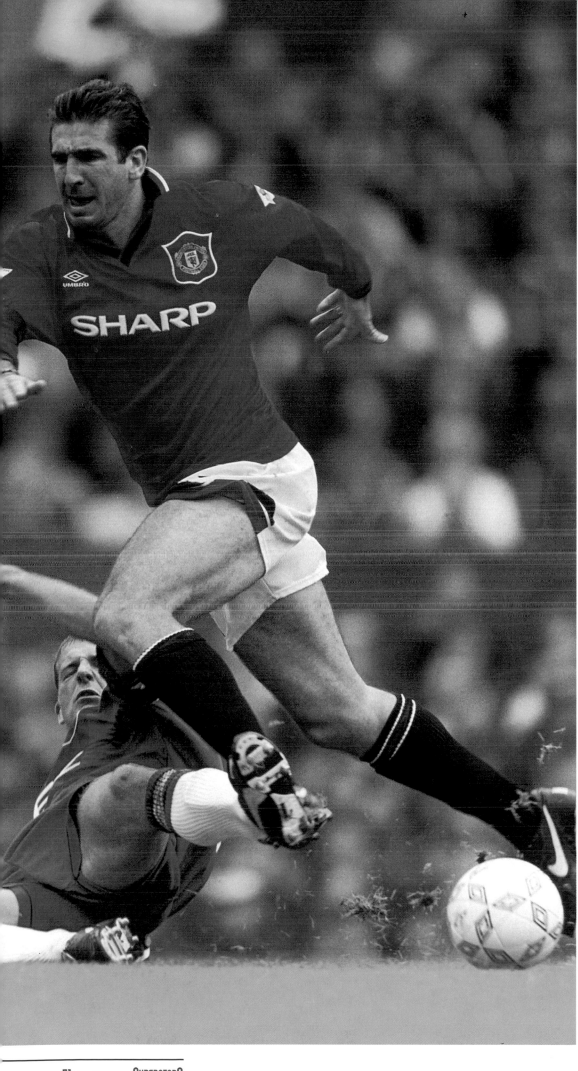

VITAL STATISTICS

Age 29

Date of Birth 24.5.1966

Place of Birth Paris

League Games & Goals
Auxerre 81[23]
Marseille 22[5]
Bordeaux 11[6]
Montpellier 33[10]
Marseille 18[8]
Nimes 17[2]
Leeds United 28[9]
Manchester United 77[39]

Honours
French Championship
1990/91 [Marseille]
First Division Championship
1991/92 [Leeds]
Premiership 1992/93,
1993/94
FA Cup 1994

Transfers
Auxerre to Marseille
[£2,200,000]
Bordeaux [loan]
Marseille to Nimes
[£1,000,000]
Nimes to Leeds [£900,000]
Leeds to Man Utd
[£1,200,000]

Position/Role
Making passes that lesser
players can't even see,
let alone hit

**Word most often
used to describe him**
Fantastique

**Word(s) never used
to describe him**
Calm and collected

Andy Cole:
expensive, but a
better player now than
ever before.

In Newcastle people may not remember the day John F Kennedy was shot, but absolutely everyone knows where they were and what they were doing when they found out Andy Cole had been sold to Manchester United.

Andy Cole had scored an incredible 55 goals in 70 League games in his spell at Newcastle, yet it only took a phone call and Keith Gillespie (oh yes, and £6 million quid) to get Keegan to sell. The Geordie fans were shattered.

Keegan says it was a great deal for the club and has indicated that his long-term vision for the team included a striker who would contribute more than just sticking the ball in the back of the net. If that's true then it's ironic that at United Cole has had to do exactly that. Without Cantona's visionary balls to run onto and deprived of the knock-downs and one-twos he'd have expected from the injured Mark Hughes, Cole had to play a new game - coming deep, getting wide and holding the ball up for his midfield.

As for his goalscoring, by the end of the season Britain's then most expensive player had scored 12 in 21 games for United - but he missed all the important ones. Against West Ham on the last day of the season he could have paid back his transfer fee in one fell swoop, but two or three times a goal, like the title, went begging.

But like so many players before him Cole, who started his career at Arsenal but found himself at the back of the strikers' queue behind Alan Smith, Ian Wright and Kevin Campbell, has found it hard to settle at United - the intense media attention and a calf injury (which everyone thought was the dreaded shin splints) clearly didn't help.

But Cole has scored goals everywhere he's played (from Arsenal he moved to Fulham on loan and then to Bristol City where he scored 20 goals in 41 games) and he now looks a more complete player than he ever did at St James' Park. This season, with Cantona and Giggs around to create openings for him, will be his true test at United - it's a frightening prospect.

VITAL STATISTICS

Age 23

Date of Birth 15.10.1971

Place of Birth Nottingham

League Games & Goals
Arsenal 1[0]
Fulham 13[3] loan
Bristol City 41[20]
Newcastle United 70[55]
Manchester United 21[12]

Honours
Division One Championship
1992/93 [Newcastle Utd]

Transfers
Arsenal to Fulham & Bristol City [loans]
Arsenal to Bristol City [£500,000]
Bristol City to Newcastle [£1,750,000]
Newcastle to Man Utd [£6,000,000 plus Keith Gillespie]

Position/Role
He gets the ball, he scores a goal… but only against Ipswich

Word(s) most often used to describe him
Goal king

Word never used to describe him
Defensive

AndyCole

'Eric Cantona's a great player.
But not as good as Ryan Giggs.'
Johann Cruyff, Barcelona manager.

Ryan Giggs

When Keith Gillespie started knocking on the first-team door at Old Trafford the media was quick, as always, to compare his talents with those of a certain great Manchester United winger. But this time the press proclaimed the imminent arrival not of 'the new George Best' but 'the new Ryan Giggs'.

At 21 Giggs is already an Old Trafford legend. And, despite the undoubted temptations, the signs are that Giggs has what it takes in the brain department to keep his life in order as well as what it takes in his feet to leave opposition defences in tatters.

Giggs has had his problems off the pitch over the last couple of years, but they've mainly been in the Old Trafford treatment room. The attentions of somewhat less skilful defenders have taken their toll. An ankle injury wrecked the first half of last season, then knee and hamstring problems meant he never really got into his stride.

Injury problems aside, Giggs's admirers are many. Early last season Barcelona boss Cruyff was asked if it was true he was trying to sign Eric Cantona. 'He's a great player,' he said, 'but not as good as Ryan Giggs.' Asked then if he wanted to sign Giggs he replied: 'Who wouldn't? Perhaps Romario, he'd hate the competition.'

The papers are full of the figures AC Milan and Barcelona are prepared to pay for him - £10 million, £12 million, £14 million. Giggs, the son of a Welsh rugby league player, says he's 'going nowhere' (hardly an appropriate phrase) and if United are to win the title back they'll need him. Ferguson's 1994/95 team without Giggs lacked the spark to unlock even Chelsea's defence (OK Cantona and Kanchelskis might have helped too), and he's as feisty as the United team that finished last season was predictable.

Oh how Terry Venables must wish he'd chosen the white of England over the red of Wales after he played for England at schoolboy level. But Giggs insists this was never on the cards. 'I only played for England schoolboys because I was at school in England,' he says.

Another sensible answer from a nice guy with more talent than most of us could ever dream of...

VITAL STATISTICS

Age 21

Date of Birth 29.11.1973

Place of Birth Cardiff

League Games & Goals
Manchester United 144[26]

94/95 League bookings
3

Ryan Giggs' 94/95 season
Giggs played in 29 League games, showed his best when he played with Cantona (who was mysteriously unavailable from January onwards), scored just one goal and was thought by many to be 'struggling for form'

Honours
Rumbelows Cup 1992
Premiership 1992/93 & 1993/94
FA Cup 1994

Position/Role
Outrageous winger, hearthrob and level-headed superstar

Word(s) most used to describe him
Level headed

Word never used to describe him
English

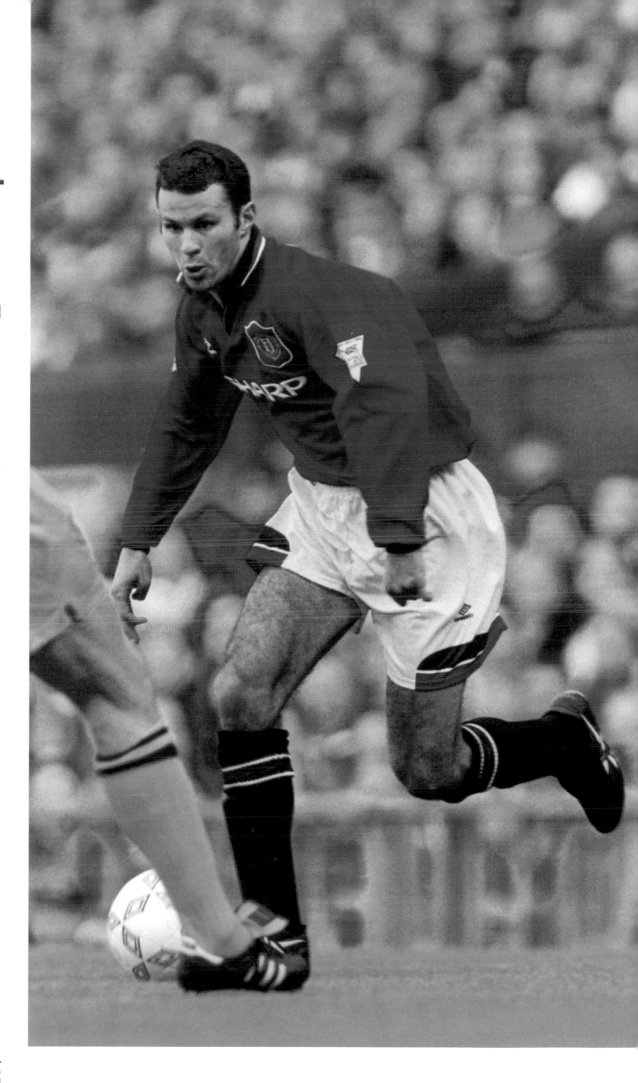

'Schmeichel is the best
I've ever seen.'
Steve Bruce, Man United's
abused captain.

Peter

Peter Schmeichel's face turns from snowy white to fluorescent purple. He turns on Steve Bruce and proceeds to hurl a torrent of garbled Scandinavian abuse at the United skipper (Danish blue?). Why? The giant keeper's just sliced a goal-kick straight into touch, that's why.

Strange antics maybe, but like all great keepers Schmeichel doesn't exactly go in for your run-of-the-mill rational behaviour.

'I don't care if he screams and bawls,' claims Bruce (Alex Ferguson once said of the pair's on-field rows: 'They're like a couple of fishwives'). But Bruce reckons, 'it's his way of concentrating' and insists, 'Schmeichel is the best I've ever seen'.

Most United fans wholeheartedly agree and since his bargain basement £550,000 move from Brondby in the summer of 1991, replacing the ever popular Les Sealey, he's provided the rock-solid foundations for four years of United success.

And although it would be churlish to blame United's relinquishing of the Premiership title to Blackburn on Schmeichel's early season injury problems, the conclusion of his record-breaking 94-game run in the team was a blow of David May blunder-like proportions to the champions. He's just so important to United. This made Gary Walsh's Nou Camp nightmare in the Champions League even harder to swallow, especially with the cheeky Spanish TV director continually cutting to a shot of a certain blond gentleman in the crowd.

With hands the size of Jutland, an XXXL-sized frame that swallows up the goal and the kind of super-confidence needed to dominate a Premiership penalty area, Schmeichel's got the lot. He's the best United keeper ever, and that's according to the official statistics not Steve Bruce. Of the 75 goalkeepers ever to play for the Red Devils, Schmeichel has the best goals-against average of any of them at just 0.79 a game. And if you toss his colossal 'defence to attack' throws, which Alex Ferguson has described as 'like Glenn Hoddle passes', into the equation then he's probably just about their best ever midfielder as well.

VITAL STATISTICS

Age 31

Date of Birth 18.11.1963

Place of Birth
Glodstone, Denmark

League Games & Goals
Manchester United 154

94/95 League bookings
0

Honours
Rumbelows Cup 1992
Premiership 1992/3,
1993/4 FA Cup 1994

Transfers
Brondby to Man Utd
[£550,000]

Position/Role
Anywhere within bellowing
distance of his defenders

Word most often
used to describe him
Outraged

Word(s) never used
to describe him
Tongue-tied

Schmeichel

Captain Marvel and the
Middlesbrough
Marvelettes are
Premiership-bound.

In true comic-book hero style, Captain Marvel became Manager Marvel and Bryan Robson led Middlesbrough back to the Premier League in his first year in control at the club. And he did it by leading the promotion push in the only way he knows how... by example.

The never-say-die attitude of the former England captain means his 38-year-old legs have had more injuries than you'll see in a whole series of *Casualty*. But they're still going strong, and you're likely to see Robson in action in the Premiership next season - if he picks himself.

'I always enjoy playing, and I'm really looking forward to playing against the top teams in the Premiership after a year in the First Division,' he says. 'But I'll only put my name on the team sheet if I know that I can still do the team justice.'

Can you imagine him doing anything else? Whether in the red of Manchester United or the white of England, Robson could always be relied upon to be an astute passer of the simple ball, a pitbull tackler, and a visionary off-the-ball runner. And he was always on hand in the box when needed to score a vital goal at one end or equally to save one with a vital tackle at the other.

But age shall wither even the best of players, and at 38 surely we can't expect to see the Robbo of old in the Premiership this season. 'My game has changed over the years,' says the veteran of 500 plus League appearances with West Brom, United and Boro. 'As you get older you tend to sit back a bit more and get a little more defensive minded, and I'm no exception. I make fewer runs into the opposition penalty box and take fewer risks. Now I concentrate on not giving the ball away.'

He'll have to concentrate pretty hard for Middlesbrough to make the grade in the top flight. And extra hard as he needs to combine his playing skills with a managerial role. 'I haven't found it at all difficult to marry management with playing,' he contests. 'Obviously I can't shout at myself in the dressing room if I've had a stinker, but I rely on my assistant Viv Anderson to do that. He'll shout at me if he feels like shouting, no worries.'

Robson being Robson, you get the feeling it's not likely to be that common an occurence.

Age 38

Date of Birth 11.1.1957

Place of Birth Chester-Le-Street

League Games & Goals
West Bromwich Albion 198[39]
Manchester United 345[74]
Middlesbrough 22[1]

Honours
Premiership 1992/93, 1993/94
League Cup 1992
FA Cup 1983, 1985, 1990, 1994

Transfers
WBA to Man Utd [£1,500,000]
Man Utd to Middlesbrough [free]

Position/Role
Box to box midfield general and caped crusader extraordinaire

Word used most often to describe him
Marvellous

Word never used to describe him
Slacker

Bryan Robson

Just about the most consistent defender in the Premier League.

In a league dominated by crops and crew cuts, blond bombshell Warren Barton stands out. But that's because of his current form, not his current hair-do.

Wimbledon's fair haired Player of the Season was just about the most consistent defender in the whole Premier League last time out as Newcastle showed by signing him in the summer. He was also about the most consistent midfielder - as anyone who plumped for Barton in their fantasy football team found out. You won't see many defenders credited with 15 'assists'.

Barton insists his best position is right-back but Wimbledon manager Joe Kinnear disagrees. 'He's too good a player to waste,' says Kinnear who played him on the right side of midfield or as a right-sided 'wing-back' in a five-man defence for most of the season.

For though Barton is as solid as they come at the back, it's when he's got the ball at his feet and there's a gap down the right that he truly blossoms with powerful swashbuckling runs, his interplay with the midfield and his pinpoint crosses.

'I had a good year,' admits Barton a few days before joining the England squad for the summer tournament against Brazil, Japan and Sweden in which, in the absence of Rob Jones, he was Terry Venables' first choice right back. 'But the whole team played well,' he adds typically.

'I just want to keep playing well and stay in the England squad. It's been a fantastic step up for me. I've had a taste of pulling on an England shirt and I want more, especially with the European Championships coming up.'

Plucked from Maidstone United (where he played 42 times) for £350,000, Barton plied his honest trade at Wimbledon for five years. Now he's an England player and the move to Newcastle 'with defence being the best form of attack and all that', at £4 million Warren Barton might just turn out to be the bargain of the season.

Warren Barton

Age **26**

Date of Birth **19.3.1969**

Place of Birth **London**

League Games & Goals
Maidstone United 42[0]
Wimbledon 180[10]

94/95 League bookings
4

Warren Barton's 94/95 season
He played 39 times for Wimbledon in the League, scored just two goals but was awarded Man of the Match an incredible 13 times.

Transfers
Orient to Leytonstone [free]
Leytonstone to Maidstone Utd [£10,000]
Maidstone to Wimbledon [£300,000]
Wimbledon to Newcastle [£4,000,000]

Position/Role
Bombing up and down the right flank doing Goldilocks impressions

Word(s) most often used to describe him
Natural blonde

Word never used to describe him
Dark

Once again, Peter Beardsley
is the toast of the Toon.

t's 1984 and Newcastle are playing Brighton and Hove Albion
in the second division. A Brighton defender is running with
the ball in his penalty box. Bad mistake with Peter Beardsley
around. Beardsley comes sliding in, comes out of the tackle
with the ball at his feet, sees Joe Corrigan rushing towards him
and, as he's getting up, chips the man-mountain keeper. The
ball hangs an age in the air and drops where it's intended to
go. Into the goal.

The little striker had signed for his home team for
£120,000 at the beginning of a marvellous season when he
teamed up with Kevin Keegan and Chris Waddle in one of the
most potent strikeforces ever put together. He hasn't looked
back since. And at 34, back in the England set-up and once
again the toast of the Toon, his career looks as bright as ever.

'You wonder what he's on, the way he races around,'
says Mark Jensen, editor of Newcastle fanzine *The Mag*.
'Although he had the odd dip in form last season, so did the
whole team, and he looks as good now as ever. He's looked
after himself.'

Beardsley has lost none of his appetite for the game
either: and he's got some appetite. 'I was at the training
ground the other day,' says Jensen, 'and the players had a day
off. Not Peter Beardsley though. He was having a training
match with the 14 to 15 year olds at the club. And he was
putting as much into that kickaround as he puts into a match.'

Gary Lineker cited Beardsley as the best partner he
ever played with in the England team. With his tenacity, his
verve, his swerving runs and the way he plays like it's his ball
and he won't let anyone else have a go... until they're in a
good shooting position, that is. You've got to think that if
Graham Taylor hadn't preferred the likes of Carlton Palmer,
Geoff Thomas and Andy Gray, England might just have been
playing in America last year. Unless Beardsley's legs tire consid-
erably in the forthcoming season, El Tel is unlikely to make the
same blunder.

Peter Beardsley

Age 34

Date of Birth 18.1.1961

Place of Birth Newcastle

League Games & Goals
   Carlisle 102[22]
   Vancouver Whitecaps
   Manchester United 0[0]
   Newcastle 147[61]
   Liverpool 131[46]
   Everton 81[25]
   Newcastle 69[33]

Honours
   First Division Championship
   1987/88, 1989/90
   FA Cup 1989 (Liverpool)

Transfers
   Carlisle to Vancouver
   Whitecaps [£275,000]
   Vancouver to Man Utd
   [£300,000]
   Man Utd to Vancouver
   [free]
   Vancouver to Newcastle
   [£150,000]
   Newcastle to Liverpool
   [£1,900,000]
   Liverpool to Everton
   [£1,000,000]
   Everton to Newcastle
   [£1,400,000]

Position/Role
   Scampering about proving
   you don't have to look good
   to play good

**Word most often
used to describe him**
   Little

**Word never used
to describe him**
   Sexy

'Shearer was good.
But Ferdinand was better.'
Chris Perry, Wimbledon
central defender.

Les

es Ferdinand is recognised as the most complete striker in the Premiership by just about everyone... except himself.

This summer's second most sought-after striker reckons he spent too much of last season 'drifting in and out of games'. OK Les, anything you say, but when you did deign to 'drift in' you just happened to smack in 24 goals and run just about every Premiership defence into the ground.

Young Wimbledon central defender Chris Perry felt the full brunt of Ferdinand during QPR's 3-1 defeat of the Dons at Selhurst Park last season. He says: 'I played against Shearer a couple of weeks before and he was good. But Ferdinand was better, outstanding, he was just so strong and quick. He really ran us ragged.'

A late starter in professional football terms - he was signed by QPR from non-league Hayes way back in 1987 but has only started to truly flourish as a striker in the last three or four years - Ferdinand doesn't have age on his side. He does have strength, touch and finishing ability which have earned him 70 League goals for Rangers in 163 games and seven England caps. These included one World Cup qualifier against Poland after which then manager Graham Taylor described Ferdinand's display as 'the most complete performance from a striker I have ever seen'.

Ferdinand's got it all. He's a lethal finisher (in the air or on the deck, inside the box or outside it), he's deadly running onto a through ball with his awesome pace but he can also come and collect the ball, turn, or hold up the play. That's how he got a price tag of £6 million. That's why Ray Wilkins and the QPR players and fans were so desperate for him to stay. Rangers have built a fine young team but without Ferdinand they have no focus.

Ferdinand, however, is now focused at Newcastle, where more is expected of him than ever before. But he's as relaxed and confident a character off the pitch as he is on it, and with better service he can only become an even better player. Sorry, keepers.

VITAL STATISTICS

Age 28

Date of Birth 18.12.1966

Place of Birth London

League Games & Goals
  QPR 163[70]

94/95 League sendings-off
  1

94/95 League bookings
  5

Transfers
  Hayes to QPR [£15,000]
  Besiktas, Turkey [loan]
  QPR to Newcastle [£6,000,000]

Position/Role
  Picking the ball up, sticking it in the net then looking mildly pleased

Word most often used to describe him
  Deadly

Word never used to describe him
  Lesley

Ferdinand

Keith Gillespie:
'I've got absolutely
no doubts I made the
right decision.'

Keith

February 19th, 1995, St James' Park. Newcastle United are battling with Manchester City for a place in the FA Cup quarter-finals. New signing Keith Gillespie gets the ball and tears down the right wing. Team-mate Paul Kitson is about five yards offside. The flag goes up. City's defence falters but the referee turns a blind eye. City defender David Brightwell manages to recover and get hold of the ball, but his back pass leaves keeper Dibble with virtually no time to get rid of it and in the resulting confusion it falls straight to Gillespie, who knocks it into the net. The 20-year-old Northern Irish international has opened his account for his new club, the first of a brace that day and, you feel, a ton over the next few seasons. City manager Brian Horton fumed about the refereeing after the game, and it wasn't the first time in February that Gillespie had quietly profited from a controversial decision. As the 'million pound makeweight' in the deal that took Andy Cole to Manchester United, he stepped out of Ryan Giggs' shadow and straight into regular first-team football while everyone else went frantic over the £6 million move the other way.

'I've got absolutely no doubts that I made the right decision,' he said towards the end of the season. 'You only had to sense the atmosphere in our 3-3 draw with Spurs to know this was a big club. The noise made by the crowd was out of this world.'

Even the disillusionment of Andrei Kanchelskis - who had been keeping him out of the United side - hasn't dissuaded him that his step across the country was in the right direction. 'You can't wonder what might have been,' he says. 'I could have been in the reserves at Old Trafford instead of playing first-team football at a terrific club.' Newcastle manager Kevin Keegan clearly believes he's a huge prospect, insisting that the Cole deal would never have gone through if it hadn't included the young winger.

As for the extra exposure, it hasn't been bad for Gillespie's international prospects or for his bank balance. He's just signed a lucrative three-year contract with Adidas to wear Predator boots. Looks like life after United is going to blossom for Gillespie... at United.

VITAL STATISTICS

Age 20

Date of Birth 18.2.1975

Place of Birth Larne, N Ireland

League Games & Goals
 Wigan 8[4]
 Manchester United 8[1]
 Newcastle United 17[2]

94/95 League bookings
 4

Keith Gillespie's 94/95 season
 Played 9 times for Man Utd, (1 goal). Played 17 times for Newcastle (2 goals)

Transfers
 Man Utd to Wigan [loan]
 Man Utd to Newcastle [part of Andy Cole transfer, valued at £1,000,000]

Position/Role
 Tricky winger and catalyst of outrageous transfer deals

Word(s) most often used to describe him
 Quick mover

Word(s) never used to describe him
 Andy Cole

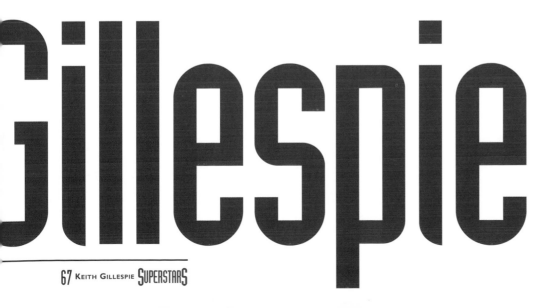

Gillespie

'He's a winner...'
Bobby Gould.

When Frank Clark took over at Forest he needed a new suit, a top-class striker and a replacement for Nigel Clough - but most of all he needed Stuart Pearce.

It may have taken a big-money contract to keep him, but Clark knew holding onto the club's 'psycho' skipper might just mean the difference between a year in the Endsleigh or a decade.

Pearce signed, missed just two games in Forest's promotion year (scoring six goals) and revelled in the battle back to the top where everyone at his first club, non-league Wealdstone FC, always knew he'd end up.

'Stuart was always a special player,' recalls Wealdstone's programme editor Roy Couch, who watched most of his 200 plus appearances for the then Southern League outfit. 'He was a quiet lad but he always stood out on the pitch, and at 17 he already had that terrific shot.'

Bobby Gould noticed him too. It took the legendary star-of-the-future-spotter and then Coventry manager just eight minutes to make up his mind about signing him on a cold, wet night at Yeovil.

'Stuart was playing for Wealdstone and it was a horrible evening,' recalls Gould. 'We'd driven half the day to get there and I was sat with my wife in the front row of the stand. After about eight minutes Stuart tackled the right winger who literally landed on my lap. That was all I needed to see and I got up to go. The wife couldn't believe it, she kept saying: "But we've only been here eight minutes."

'It's his competitiveness that makes him the player he is,' says Gould. 'It's the strength of his mind as much as the strength of his left foot. He's a winner and he always knows where he's going, where he wants to be.'

Gould believes Pearce could have made a name for himself as a left-sided midfielder and was seriously considering playing him there at the beginning of the 1983/84 campaign before the future England skipper got injured with shin splints and missed half the season. By mid-season Coventry were bottom of the League and Gould was sacked. 'He cost me my job,' says Gould. He might just have saved Frank Clark's.

VITAL STATISTICS

Age 33

Date of Birth 24.4.1962

Place of Birth London

League Games & Goals
Coventry City 52[4]
Nottingham Forest 337[8]

94/95 League bookings
7

Honours
League Cup 1989,1990
FA Cup Runners-up 1991

Transfers
Wealdstone to Coventry
[£25,000]
Coventry to Forest
[£200,000]

Position/Role
On the left with his shorts pulled up too high, looking for someone to tackle

Word most often used to describe him
Killer

Word never used to describe him
Wimp

StuartPearce

Bryan Roy:
Quick-footed, quick-witted
and, er, quick.

Just when he's about to set the world on fire, Bryan Roy seems to let off his personal fire extinguisher and douse the flames. For years it seems Roy has been billed as the super-talented saviour of Dutch football in waiting, yet - despite some magnificent performances - we're still waiting.

At times last season he was majestic for Forest. Running at defences and shooting on sight, he had the swagger of a true great. At other times you wondered if he was still on the pitch.

Roy started the campaign like he hadn't played for years, but by mid-season he was on the receiving end of a 'poor workrate' public blasting from Frank Clark. Roy's fitness was obviously deemed to be the problem because, not long afterwards, he was spotted running along the banks of the Trent in a special suit loaded with weights. Yet by the end of the campaign he was at it again, scoring from 30 yards and missing sitters like all true greats.

'One of the reasons Roy is so popular with Forest fans is because, if he's not playing well, at least he'll put up his hand and admit it,' says Andy Lowe, editor of Forest fanzine *The Tricky Tree*. 'He went in for extra training after Frank Clark had a go at him. Collymore went into a strop and slagged off his team-mates.'

All through his career Bryan Roy has been the genius who's yet to blossom. Stuck out on the wing at his first club Ajax, they said he'd never fulfil his potential and sold him to Italian club Foggia. There, given a free role in the middle of the field, he played the best football of his career but, whenever he pulled on the orange shirt of Holland, it didn't quite happen - he spent most of USA 94 on the bench, used only as a second-half sub.

After his £2.5 million move to Forest, though, he set off like a steam train, playing in the middle behind Collymore - a role he'd insisted on before signing. Quick-footed, quick-witted and, er, quick, he's got everything. If he could ever sustain his best form for a season or so then we would be talking about a truly great footballer. Forest fans don't mind one bit if he hangs around on the off-chance.

Bryan Roy

VITAL STATISTICS

Age 25

Date of Birth 12.2.1970

Place of Birth Amsterdam

League Games & Goals
Ajax 103[17]
Foggia 25[11]
Nottingham Forest 37[13]

94/95 League bookings
4

Bryan Roy's 94/95 season
Played 37 times in the
League for Forest, scoring
13 times. Contributed
strikingly to Forest's
surprise finish of 3rd in
the Premiership

Transfers
Foggia to Forest
[£2,500,000]

Position/Role
Displaying outrageous skills
then hiding in Jason Lee's
hair-do

**Word most often
used to describe him**
Tease

**Word(s) never used
to describe him**
Rover-like

'I hope he makes it to the top, but I'd like it to be with us.'
Ray Wilkins, QPR player-manager.

Honesty and loyalty. Not the adjectives that normally spring to mind when talking about your average footballer. Trevor Sinclair, it seems, is different.

Chased by a whole host of clubs while playing schoolboy football in Oldham, he signed for unglamorous Blackpool. Approached by Blackburn when on the verge of completing a deal with QPR, he turned down Rovers' riches and signed for Rangers anyway. 'I had already given Gerry Francis my word,' he said. And when asked, after scoring the winner in England's Under-21 game against Latvia, if he was looking to break into the full England squad soon, he replied: 'I think that's a bit optimistic. We've started a job in the Under-21s and we have a good chance of reaching the European finals. I'd like to see it through.'

'He's a really nice lad,' confirms Blackpool's youth team coach Neil Bailey who took charge of 16-year-old Sinclair when he came out of the FA's School of Excellence at Lilleshall. 'He's always smiling, he's always got a twinkle in his eye. He's really bright and bubbly and that's how he plays his football.'

Following his £600,000 transfer to QPR after making 112 League appearances (scoring 15 times) for Blackpool, Sinclair has replaced Andy Sinton's wing trickery and made it a distant memory for Rangers fans. Be it buzzing around on either wing, playing as an out-and-out striker or slotting in behind the front two, he's trouble for any defence. A finely tuned athlete, he's good in the air as well as with the ball at his feet and last season he notched four goals to help QPR to the lofty heights of ninth in the Premiership.

QPR fans won't thank anyone for saying it, but 'Where next?' is the phrase people associate with Trevor Sinclair these days. 'I hope he makes it to the top but I would like it to be with us,' says Ray Wilkins.

And whatever is in store for his former prodigy, Neil Bailey won't be surprised: 'When you see ability like Trevor Sinclair had as a youngster then you know you're watching something special.'

Trevor Sinclair

Chris Bart-Williams didn't make the Sheffield Wednesday team defeated so narrowly by Arsenal in the 1993 FA Cup final, but it was during that match that the rap-loving midfielder got his nickname. Picture this. The TV camera flashes to the Wednesday bench and Owls manager Trevor Francis is up on his feet, willing his men forward, screaming blue murder. Behind him is Bart-Williams, sitting calmly in his suit, bopping away to his Walkman and seemingly oblivious to everything around him. The nickname? Shabba.

Not that Bart-Williams is oblivious to everything around him when he's on the pitch. The England Under-21 international has been playing regular first-team football for four years, first with Leyton Orient and for the last three seasons in the Premiership colours of Sheffield Wednesday. 'He's a very considerable talent,' says Dave Sexton, manager of the Under-21 side for whom Chris has made 16 appearances. 'He's confident on the ball and he's got good skill to go with it. What's more he's always willing to accept the ball, which is great in a youngster.'

The fans like him too. 'He's a very popular player here, but his problem is his lack of consistency,' says Peter Holmes, editor of Wednesday fanzine *A View from the East Bank*. 'But a lot of that must be down to Trevor Francis, who played him all over the place last season. He's been a winger, upfront, behind the front two, on the left and right of midfield, in a holding position... he even partnered Des Walker in central defence in a pre-season friendly. If he was left to play in one position he'd be less of an enigma. As it is, sometimes he looks brilliant, sometimes he looks lethargic and disinterested.'

There's a fine line between versatilty and jack-of-all-tradesmanship, and it looks like Bart-Williams will have to find a consistent role to fulfil all that early promise. 'He'd like to be a midfield general, but I can see his best position being behind the front two,' continues Sexton. 'If he works on his running off the ball and his heading and sticks to that position I think he could make it all the way to the senior side.' Did you hear that Shabba? DID YOU HEAR THAT SHABBA?

'He's a very considerable talent.'
Dave Sexton.

Chris Bart-Willia

VITAL STATISTICS

Age 21

Date of Birth 16.6.1974

Place of Birth Freetown, Sierra Leone

League Games & Goals
Leyton Orient 36[2]
Sheffield Wednesday 102[16]

94/95 League bookings
6

Chris Bart-Williams' 94/95 season
Played for Sheff Wed 38 times in the League, scoring twice.

Transfers
Orient to Sheff Weds [£275,000]

Position/Role
You tell him, he wouldn't mind knowing

Word most often used to describe him
Versatile

Word never used to describe him
Consistent

ns

Chris Waddle's pace and trickery could skin any defence.

t would be tempting to remember Chris Waddle as 'the man who missed the penalties' after last season's FA Cup 4th round after-extra-time fluff against Wolves brought his Italia 90 semi-final blast over the bar so clearly to mind. But that would be rotten when he's been one of the most exciting players to grace the field over the last decade.

Let's instead remember the image of Waddle in 1985, playing for Newcastle against Tottenham, all hunched shoulders and socks down to his ankles. Let's remember him receiving the ball in midfield in that game looking like a 40-Marlboro-a-day man after a marathon in Florida, lifting his head to work out his options, then doing the famous Waddle shuffle to take him past the lunging tackles of two men and curling a 25-yarder into the net. What a player.

Waddle started out playing for Newcastle in a dream attack alongside Terry McDermott, Peter Beardsley and Kevin Keegan. 'As a kid the four players I tried to be in the playground were Franny Lee, Tony Currie, Stan Bowles and Rodney Marsh. Oh, and don't forget George Best.' OK, so not many kids were trying to be Nobby Stiles, but Waddle was soon emulating these flair stylists himself at St James' Park. His pace and trickery could skin any defence... if at first his crossing was shocking.

Just as shocking, in fact, as his haircut when he moved to Tottenham in 1985. The German rucksacker look and a brief foray into the pop charts helped disguise an iffy-at-first period in north London, but Marseille had seen enough to pay £4.25 million to take him to the south of France. At Olympique he became one of the best players in Europe, just missing out on a European Cup winner's medal due to a gritty defensive display and a penalty shoot-out win by Red Star Belgrade. Waddle, for the record, declined to take one. But despite universal praise, Graham Taylor saw fit to discard him and his international career was over just as he reached his peak. Last season the injury-plagued winger was in and out of the Wednesday side but, though he performed in fits and starts, the fits were well worth waiting for.

VITAL STATISTICS

Age 35

Date of Birth 14.4.1960

Place of Birth Hepworth

League Games & Goals
Newcastle United 170[46]
Tottenham Hotspur 138[33]
Marseille 107[22]
Sheffield Wednesday 77[8]

Transfers
Tow Law to Newcastle [£1,000]
Newcastle to Tottenham [£590,000]
Tottenham to Marseille [£4,250,000]
Marseille to Sheff Wed [£1,000,000]

Position/Role
Swapping wings and missing penalties

Word(s) most often used to describe him
Diamond Light

Word never used to describe him
Hunky

Chris Waddle

N ever one to shy away from the limelight, crazy keeper Bruce Grobbelaar managed to get himself splashed all over the front pages as well as the back ones last season. But whatever the outcome of the various match-rigging accusations, Grobbelaar and his unique goalkeeping antics will never be anything but legendary among football fans.

The former Zimbabwean soldier first appeared on the English scene between the sticks (and pretty well everywhere else for that matter) for Crewe Alexandra, after a stint with Vancouver Whitecaps in Canada. In 1980 he was signed by Liverpool - to replace cardboard-cutout-in-comparison Anfield legend Ray Clemence - and English football had to sit up and take notice. You could hardly ignore him: for his breathtaking agility, his clowning around, his goal-saving charges out of the box... and for his occasional but almighty match-costing blunder.

'Every mistake Bruce makes is a positive mistake,' squeaks Alan Ball, speaking when he was still Grobbelaar's manager at Southampton, 'because Bruce is a very positive goalkeeper. He's got an enormous belief in himself and incredible single-mindedness.'

It's this single-mindedness that makes Grobbelaar charge into territory usually virgin to keepers' studmarks to clear the ball when there's danger afoot, shuttling his team's fans' hearts right into their gobs. He doesn't do this because he's lost his head. He's taking a calculated risk, assuming that he can get to the ball before the oncoming attacker. Unfortunately, like all calculated risks, a small percentage go wrong, and when you're a goalkeeper the headlines blare your blunder to the nation.

'He's calmed down a bit now anyway,' continues Ball. 'As you get older you do. Bruce has turned into the complete keeper. He's very commanding in the penalty box, which is reassuring for your defence. He's a great shot-stopper and very positive when coming out for crosses.'

Unfortunately the most difficult cross for Grobbelaar at the moment is the one he has to bear as a professional player accused of match-rigging. And, not for the first time, he'll be looking for his defence to get him out of trouble.

'He's calmed down a bit now.'
Alan Ball, Manchester City manager.

Bruce Grobbelaar

VITAL STATISTICS

Age 37

Date of Birth 6.10.1957

Place of Birth
Durban, South Africa

League Games & Goals
Crewe Alex 24[1] yes he scored!
Liverpool 440
Stoke City 4 loan
Southampton 30

Honours
Division 1 Championship
1981/82, 1982/83,
1983/84, 1985/86,
1987/88, 1989/90
European Cup 1884
FA Cup 1986, 1989, 1992
League Cup 1982, 1983,
1984

Transfers
Vancouver Whitecaps to
Crewe [free]
Crewe to Vancouver [free]
Vancouver to Liverpool
[£250,000]
Liverpool to Southampton
[free]

Position/Role
Unpredictable goalkeeper
cum left back cum clown

**Word most often
used to describe him**
Different

**Word never used
to describe him**
Boring

'In short,
he's a one-off.'
Alan Ball, Manchester
City manager.

Matt
Le

Only Matt Le Tissier can do that...' enthused John Motson as the Southampton lynchpin turned to celebrate his 'Goal of the Season', that dipping 40-yarder that caught Blackburn keeper Tim Flowers inches out of position but yards away from getting a hand to the ball, '...because only he would have thought of it!'

Commentators have come on a long way since the 'What a goal' days of Kenneth Wolstenholme, but they've got their work cut out describing the maverick wanderings of England's most naturally gifted player. 'He's one of very few players I've seen with all-round ability,' drools Alan Ball, speaking before his move to Manchester City of his delight that Le Tiss had again pledged his future to the south coast club. 'He can play it long, he can play it short. He's superbly precise in his passing, he's a magnificent manipulator and he can make and score goals. In short, he's a one-off.'

The Channel Islander first caught the eye in a Southampton youth-team attack which also included Rodney Wallace and Alan Shearer. 'Wallace had the pace, Shearer had the strength, and Le Tissier had the natural ability. And still has,' says Chris Nicholl, Saints manager at the time. Le Tissier quickly moved up a couple of grades to the first team, and it wasn't long before he was the creative focus of the side, gradually moving deeper infield from a central striking role to give him more room to manoeuvre, create and score.

'To put it in racing terms,' continues Ball, who likes putting things in racing terms, 'he's the star horse in a stable full of handicappers.' Ball was talking about the stable that he ran on the south coast, but he might as well have been talking about the whole country. If Le Tiss ever played for England the way he's played for Southampton, Terry Venables would have the key to unlock the tightest defences in the world. But there lies the Le Tissier enigma. England managers have long been suspicious of putting all their creative eggs in one basket, and Venables is no exception. So unless Le Tiss can learn more of a bit-part international role (if he's ever given another chance) he's likely to fall to the same fate as the most gifted player of the generation before him, Glenn Hoddle, who didn't win half the caps he could have, not because he wasn't good enough, but because he was too good.

VITAL STATISTICS

Age 26

Date of Birth 14.10.1966

Place of Birth Guernsey

League Games & Goals
Southampton 292[119]

94/95 League bookings
6

Matt Le Tissier's 94/95 season
Appeared in more League games than any other Southampton player - 41, scoring 19 times. Was Southampton's Man of the Match on nine occasions

Position/Role
Marauding genius on the pitch, sit-tight homelover off it

Word most often used to describe him
Indescribable

Word never used to describe him
Handsome

Tissier

'He looks ungainly, but he's extremely quick.' Gary Mabbutt, Tottenham captain.

So why do they call him Shaggy?' I ask Tottenham captain Gary Mabbutt of flying winger Darren Anderton. 'Can't you tell?' smiles Mabbutt. 'It's because he looks like the character out of Scooby Doo.'

Anderton certainly runs as fast as his cartoon counterpart, though with a ball at his feet and bearing down on the opposition defence he's more terrifying than terrified. With his beanpole stature, ruffled hair and his socks falling down, he's the antithesis of your traditional five foot nothing sixpence ha'penny winger. But in the last couple of seasons Anderton's skilful performances down the flank for Spurs have earned the former Portsmouth starlet rave reviews and a regular spot in Terry Venables' England side.

'A couple of seasons back we were very poor, and nearly got relegated,' says Mabbutt. 'But Darren shone out above the rest of the team and had an excellent season. And he played even better last season when we started to get things together a little bit.'

Everything about Anderton is long... his face, his frame, his stride. He looks like the sort of guy that would goof everything up in a park kickaround. Yet time and time again he's skinned defences to deliver a telling cross or put the ball in the back of the net himself. 'Yes, he's very deceptive,' says Mabbutt. 'In a way he's like Chris Waddle in that he looks ungainly yet he's extremely quick. He loves taking people on and beating them and he's one of the best crossers of the ball I've seen in my career. He's also got a lethal shot.'

He may not have scored for England yet, but his energetic performances wide on the right have been some of the few bright spots in Venables' first year at the helm of the England team. But has Anderton found the transition to international football as easy as he's made it look? 'It's a totally different game,' he says. 'It's not necessarily more difficult, though. You're playing against better players, sure, but you're playing with better players, too. I've enjoyed playing with Gazza, Paul Ince, David Platt. They've brought out the best in me.' But have they? Anderton's still only 23, so England and Spurs fans will be hoping 'the best' is still to come.

Darren Anderton

VITAL STATISTICS

Age 23

Date of Birth 3.3.1972

Place of Birth Southampton

League Games & Goals
Portsmouth 62[6]
Tottenham 108[17]

94/95 League bookings
3

Darren Anderton's 94/95 season
Appeared in 37 League games. He scored five times (twice at home, three times away). Was Man of the Match three times. Spent the season being overshadowed by a certain German

Transfers
Portsmouth to Tottenham [£1,750,000]

Position/Role
Roving 'boy next door' beanpole winger

Word most often used to describe him
Lanky

Word never used to describe him
Lethargic

In 1994/95, Sheringham quietly notched up another 23 goals for Spurs.

Teddu

May 14th, 1995, White Hart Lane. Klinsmann's last stand. The German bows out to his adoring fans as Tottenham gain an honourable 1-1 draw with Europe-bound Leeds. The goal? The goal is scored by Teddy Sheringham.

In a season of Klinsmann, Shearer and Cole, Teddy Sheringham quietly notched up 23 goals for Tottenham. Par for the course for the blond England international. 'He had another excellent year,' says his skipper Gary Mabbutt. 'You can guarantee that Teddy will score 20 or more goals in a season.' What about Teddymania? For all his attributes, for all his goals, Sheringham remains largely an unsung hero. Tottenham fans certainly don't moan when the former Millwall and Forest man is picked for England, but it seems everybody else does.

'He certainly deserves a chance in the England team,' says Mabbutt, no stranger to the three-lioned shirt. 'He's come on in leaps and bounds since he joined Tottenham and he's improving all the time. The thing is many people don't notice half the work he's doing. His strength is his all-round ability.'

Former Tottenham striker Garth Crooks agrees. 'Talking to some of his colleagues they tell me that he's a genuine all-round footballer, which is an enormous strength. He doesn't just have the capacity to score goals, he can make them and he can stop them. And most importantly he has presence. A defence knows he's there and assumes respect. Martin Chivers had that sort of presence. Greaves had it, Best had it, Gascoigne has it, all the great players have it... Shearer has it. It can give you an extra yard because you have respect.'

It seems Sheringham's lot, then, is to receive respect not adulation, although with Klinsmann gone he'll certainly get a bit more of the limelight. But will he miss Der Dive Bomber? 'Everybody will miss Klinsmann, especially his strike partner,' says Mabbutt. 'Any player worth their salt would miss Klinsmann,' says Crooks. 'But I bet you one thing, Klinsmann will miss Sheringham too.'

Sheringham

An international
call-up isn't totally
out of the question.

P atience is a virtue well known to West Ham's lynchpin midfielder John Moncur. Having joined Tottenham as an apprentice in 1984 he went on to make 21 appearances for the club. But even diehard Spurs fans can be forgiven for hardly remembering him. At an average of three per season, his rare appearances spanned a period of seven years!

'There were always great midfield players around at Tottenham like Ardiles, Hoddle, Gascoigne and Nayim, and I never got a look in,' he explains. Eventually John moved to Swindon in 1991, but only after unsuccesful loan periods with Cambridge United, Doncaster Rovers, Portsmouth, Brentford, Ipswich and Nottingham Forest, where he wasn't even given a game.

It was former team-mate Glenn Hoddle who rescued him and included him in the line-up of a Swindon team that won promotion to the Premiership for the first time in history. And, although he endured the nightmare of relegation the next year, at least John achieved his dream of playing a full season - and playing so well that there were a number of teams interested in keeping him in the Premiership at the end of it. Ultimately it was a toss up between West Ham and Chelsea.

'It was a dream to play in a team managed by Glenn and a lot of people assumed I would go to Chelsea,' he says, 'But my decision was a gut reaction in the end and I think they are usually the best to follow.'

Hoddle is a player who comes to mind when making comparisons with Moncur. The latter is tougher and stronger than his former Spurs colleague but has that astute sense of when to make the right pass and a penchant for drifting past tackles, attributes that were elemental in West Ham's crawl to safety last season. And if he carries on the way he's going, an international call-up isn't totally out of the question... especially as he's an ex-Spurs man.

VITAL STATISTICS

Age 28

Date of Birth 22.9.1966

Place of Birth Stepney

League Games & Goals
Tottenham 21[1]
Cambridge United 4[0] loan
Doncaster Rovers 4[0] loan
Portsmouth 7[0] loan
Brentford 5[1] loan
Ipswich 6[0] loan
Swindon 58[5]
West Ham 30[2]

Transfers
Tottenham to Cambridge & Brentford [loan]
Tottenham to Swindon [£80,000]
Swindon to West Ham [900,000]

Position/Role
Creator of chances for West Ham strikers to miss

Word(s) used most often to describe him
Well travelled

Word never used to describe him
Uncultured

John Moncur

Deano: looking forward to hitting the back of the net again.

Dea

In keeping with football's 1994/95 theme, Dean Holdsworth had a complete nightmare last season. He started the season as Wimbledon's captain, top scorer and Player of the Season and seemed on the verge of a full England call-up. Then disaster.

Injured on the club's pre-season Scandinavian tour, stripped of the captaincy and given a public crazy-gang roasting for demanding a transfer (just weeks after signing a lucrative new deal) when the club sold his striking partner John Fashanu, you could say the season didn't start well. And it didn't get better. The injury (inflammation of the sciatic nerve) got worse, the tabloids said he was faking it, the fans got on his back, the goals dried up and Holdsworth was ordered to rest.

By the end of the campaign he was back in the team but still not scoring (bad news if your contract includes a 'cash for goals' clause). It was a goal drought, and that's one thing the 26 year old had never suffered from since finding his goalscoring touch at Brentford, where he notched 76 League and Cup strikes in three seasons. 'I never go onto the pitch thinking I'm not going to score,' said Holdsworth. 'I always go out there to score, but you always need a bit of luck as well.'

And the ball, like the luck, wasn't running for a striker not known for his pace but usually lethal given the slightest sniff of a chance in the box. No doubt Deano was missing the scraps that Fashanu's hustling and bustling fed to him the year before, but nothing went his way until the last game of the season, when a clinically taken half-chance and a confident penalty against Forest gave an inkling that the Deano of old was lurking in that blue shirt somewhere.

Now he's patched up his differences with Wimbledon, withdrawn his transfer request and is looking forward to hitting the back of the net again.

'If I can start scoring goals again then I'd like to get back in the international reckoning,' he insists. 'I aim to stay at the top.'

VITAL STATISTICS

Age 26

Date of Birth 8.11.1968

Place of Birth London

League Games & Goals
Watford 16[3]
Carlisle 4[1] loan
Port Vale 6[2] loan
Swansea 5[1] loan
Brentford 7[1] loan
Brentford 110[53]
Wimbledon 87[43]

Transfers
Watford to Carlisle &
Swansea [loans]
Watford to Brentford
[£125,000]
Brentford to Wimbledon
[£720,000]

Position/Role
Ambling around with his
shirt hanging out... until
he gets half a chance

**Word most often
used to describe him**
Sniffer

**Word never used
to describe him**
Playmaker

Holdsworth

Predictions for the Premier

With 760 matches to be played in the Premiership this season, not even the largest, most complex computer could work out how the League table might look at the end of the season. So we sat down with a cup of tea and a packet of jaffas and worked it out for ourselves...

Predicted final table 1995/96

1	Manchester Utd	6	Notts Forest	11	Arsenal	16	Wimbledon
2	Leeds	7	Tottenham	12	Aston Villa	17	Bolton
3	Blackburn	8	Chelsea	13	Coventry	18	Middlesborough
4	Liverpool	9	Everton	14	Southampton	19	Sheffield Wed
5	Newcastle	10	QPR	15	Manchester City	20	West Ham

Arsenal

If Big Brother was an Arsenal fan he'd be down the Ministry of Truth having the whole of the 1994/95 season erased from history right now. Only poor old Arsenal's season could carry on being disastrous even after it had finished ('mmmnn, a quiet end of season trip to the Far East is just what we need to put our troubles behind us'). Can the Gunners get back to firing on all four cylinders with Bruce Rioch, a geriatric defence and seventeen decidedly average midfielders? The answer is yes, eventually.
Prediction 11th

Aston Villa

Okay so they're getting on a bit, but on paper Villa have a side that should be challenging for honours every season. But football is played on grass and mud and last season Brian Little's team nearly found themselves face first in it, not making good their escape from the drop until the very last game. This season surely won't find them in as much trouble, but Little's got his work cut out over the summer trying to instil some sort of *esprit de corps* among the team. Don't expect fireworks, but it can't be as bad as last year.
Prediction 12th

Blackburn

Despite the magnificence of Alan Shearer, what ultimately clinched the title for Kenny Dalglish's team last year was a kung fu kick at Selhurst Park. Worthy, hard-working, quick and strong are the adjectives most often applied to the Lancashire team, but surely such attributes are not enough to forge a 'Blackburn era' in English football. Maybe Jack Walker's cheque book will pay the way for a tad more craft to go with the graft, but it won't be enough to retain the title.
Prediction 3rd

League

Bolton

They've done the easy bit, now the real battle starts. There's no doubt Bolton deserved their Premiership place but keeping it is going to be another matter. With quality players like McAteer, Lee, McGinlay and Stubbs - if they can hold on to them - they're certainly better equipped to deal with coming up from the play-offs than Swindon or Leicester City were. No-one will fancy the trip to Burnden Park so their away form will be the key. A few wins and they'll stay up.
Prediction 17th

Chelsea

Last season saw a spirited but doomed Chelsea effort in the Cup Winners' Cup. This season sees the arrival of Ruud 'I've always admired Glenn' Gullit. Nevertheless, expect some fine football from old rasta-head who, at 33, has still got what it takes to fill stadiums and play at the top. Once you've got over the shock of seeing him in a Chelsea shirt, it should be a sight to behold. And Mark Hughes should be good for a few goals, even though his best days are gone.
Prediction 8th

Coventry

If you wanted someone to liven up a party you'd ask Big Ron over. But there hadn't been a party at Coventry City since they won the FA Cup in 1987 so Atkinson had to start one all on his own. No problem. He brought master magician Gordon Strachan with him to Highfield Road to do a few tricks and now, all of a sudden, everyone's smiling. Okay City aren't going to win the League, but with quality players like Ndlovu, Dublin, Richardson and Burrows on call there's no reason why the festivities need to end just yet.
Prediction 13th

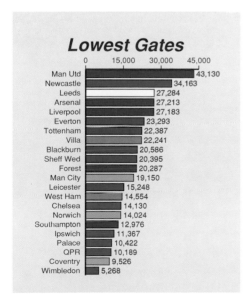

Lowest Gates

Man Utd	43,130
Newcastle	34,163
Leeds	27,284
Arsenal	27,213
Liverpool	27,183
Everton	23,293
Tottenham	22,387
Villa	22,241
Blackburn	20,586
Sheff Wed	20,395
Forest	20,287
Man City	19,150
Leicester	15,248
West Ham	14,554
Chelsea	14,130
Norwich	14,024
Southampton	12,976
Ipswich	11,367
Palace	10,422
QPR	10,189
Coventry	9,526
Wimbledon	5,268

What will be the smallest gate at your ground this year? This is what happened last season.

Everton

The stressometer will go off the dial in the blue half of Liverpool if Everton put their fans through a third season of relegation-battling woe this time. Winning the FA Cup may do wonders for morale and it seems there's money available for players. Joe Royle certainly seems to know where he's going - but Everton are a million miles away from being a major force in the game again. Still, Captain Royle is steering them in the right direction and it looks like calmer waters ahead.
Prediction 9th

Leeds

One man made all the difference to Leeds' fortunes last year, and his name was Tony Yeboah. Pre-Yeboah, United were all over the place and a non-entity of a season was on the cards. Post-Yeboah they soared into a place in Europe. This season Leeds will be sporting the no-frills all-white kit like the one they wore in the glory days of the 1970s and having managed to keep hold of the big Ghanaian for at least another year, they could just start to emulate that great Revie-run side. A force to be reckoned with.
Prediction 2nd

Liverpool

The Roy Evans revival show marches on but the good old days still seem a long, long way off at Anfield. Liverpool are a good side but some way from being a great one and the title is surely out of reach again this year. The current blend of youth and experience has knitted the team together well but, more often than not, the football's all very pretty but going nowhere. Still, the addition of a couple of new faces could change that very suddenly indeed.
Prediction 4th

Middlesbrough

Bryan Robson's boys deservedly won the Endsleigh First Division last season, but it must be said that they were the best of a bad lot, losing nearly a quarter of their games. Marvel Manager Robson is hailing the dawning of a new era on Teeside and how he'd love to emulate neighbour Kevin Keegan and see his rookies challenging for honours in the first season back at the top. But we're not likely to see much of Robson on the pitch and, with the gulf between divisions widening by the season, Middlesbrough are likely to be too close to the other end of the table for comfort.
Prediction 18th (relegated)

Manchester City

Oh brother! The only thing that Man City fans had to cheer about last season was the last week of United's season. Despite the Blues' deadly attack (Summerbee and Beagrie down the wings, Walsh and Rosler through the middle) they only just escaped the dreaded drop... again. There's little to suggest that City's fortunes will change much in the coming season. Sure they'll get enough good results to keep them up but, come May, they're more likely to be looking over their shoulder at the Endsleigh than making a sprint for Europe.
Prediction 15th

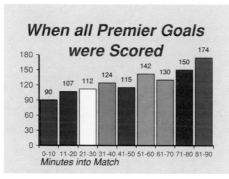

Last season's goal tally.

Newcastle

Despite the massive presence of the Toon Army at Newcastle's away games last year, Kevin Keegan's pop-gun side only won one match on the road after September... and although they'll be almost impregnable again at Fortress St James', they'll have to improve on their travels to hope to get into Europe. The return of Philip 'Prince' Albert should bolster up their Keystone Cops defence, however, and with Scott Sellars back on the left a place in the UEFA Cup should be won by the end of the season, especially now Keegan has Ferdinand in his armoury.
Prediction 5th

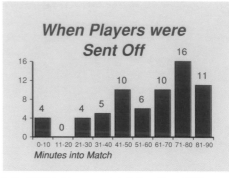

In the 94/95 season, you were pretty safe committing a foul in the 12th minute.

Manchester United

'This will make us stronger,' said Alex Ferguson ominously in May as his butter-fingers side let both the Premiership title and the FA Cup slip in the space of six days. Even without Cantona, Giggs and Kanchelskis, United should have won the League last season and, frankly, you can't see the red machine spluttering again this time out. Without the pressure of the European Cup, and with a clutch of youngsters with a year's worth of experience under their belts, they've probably just put an 'on loan' sign where the Premiership trophy sat at Old Trafford.
Prediction 1st

Nottingham Forest

Wham bam thank you Stan. It was short but it sure was sweet, but what sort of punch will Forest without Collymore pack? The feeling in Nottingham is not that the man will be hard to replace, more that he's irreplaceable. Still, it's not all doom and gloom with a squad jam-packed full of talent and presumably with roughly £8.5 million in the coffers. Bryan Roy may hold the key and a lot will rest on his talented but erratic shoulders. Life goes on and Forest will be OK.
Prediction 6th

QPR

It's the same old story at QPR. A nice ground, some good players, a decent young manager who likes his team to play football. There are usually a few goals at either end at Loftus Road but never any trophies in the cabinet at the end of the season. Give him a couple of years without selling anyone and Ray Wilkins might change all that, but at the moment it looks like another mid-table season but plenty of thrills and spills... again.
Prediction 10th

Sheffield Wednesday

The Owls could struggle to keep their place in the top flight this season. There won't be much room in the new pint-sized Premiership for inconsistent sides and Wednesday, who lacked a killer instinct all last season, may struggle. At least they'll grace the Endsleigh League if they do go down.
Prediction 19th (relegated)

Southampton

It's tempting to attribute Southampton's safe mid-table position last season (instead of the usual skin-of-the-teeth relegation escape) entirely to the gifted boots of Matthew Le Tissier. But that would be a rather shallow analysis. Le Tiss is the team's lynchpin, sure, and with 28 goals to his credit, by far the highest scorer in the south coast side. But Alan Ball has got a wise footballing brain on his shoulders and surrounded the Channel Islander with a skilful cohesive unit, changing Branfoot's carthorse to a sleek flat-runner. Expect the Saints to fade.
Prediction 14th

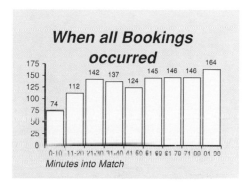

Last season's yellow card fever.

Wimbledon

No ground, no money and no Warren Barton. Yet again the Dons start a season as relegation certainties but this season really could be Wimbledon's toughest test for a while. Barton's loss will make a sluggish defence that still misses John Scales even shakier, and the front men will miss the blond bomber's marauding service down the right flank as well. Selhurst Park gives them no home advantage and with the new Homesdale Road stand it'll be even eerier on Wimbledon home match days. It's gonna be a difficult season, but when the going gets tough...
Prediction 16th

Tottenham

And it was all going so well... Spurs had found Gerry and Gerry had found the formula to make Spurs tick, and win, without spending a penny. Then Klinsmann dropped his 'opt-out clause' bombshell and Tottenham are looking like a team that might struggle again. OK they've only lost one player but, if they had to lose anyone... Will Alan Sugar part with any more dosh? Will Barmby and Rosenthal be able to fill the goalscoring gap left by Jurgen the German? Will Spurs ever mount a serious title challenge? Not this year.
Prediction 7th

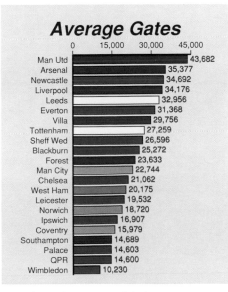

Where do most fans go on match day?

West Ham

In the new streamlined Premiership there will be no room for also-rans and, despite their pretty ball-to-feet football style, this Hammers side does not look good enough to survive among the big boys, despite the fine distribution of John Moncur in the middle of the field and some raucous support at Upton Park.
Prediction 20th (relegated)

1994/95 Premier League

Top Goalscorers

Alan Shearer	34
Robbie Fowler	26
Les Ferdinand	24
Stan Collymore	22
Matt Le Tissier	20
Jurgen Klinsmann	20
Ian Wright	18
Teddy Sheringham	18
Uwe Rosler	15
Dean Saunders	15
Chris Sutton	15

Top 10 'Leaky defences'

Ipswich (conceded)	93
Leicester	80
Wimbledon	65
Manchester City	64
Southampton	63
Coventry	62
QPR	59
Tottenham	58
Sheffield Wednesday	57
Aston Villa	56

Highest Gates

Man Utd	43,868
Villa	40,154
Liverpool	40,014
Everton	40,011
Leeds	39,396
Arsenal	39,377
Newcastle	35,626
Sheff Wed	34,051
Tottenham	33,040
Chelsea	31,161
Blackburn	30,545
Forest	28,882
Man City	27,850
West Ham	24,783
Ipswich	22,559
Coventry	21,885
Norwich	21,843
Leicester	21,393
QPR	18,948
Palace	18,224
Wimbledon	18,224
Southampton	15,210

Top 10 'Bore draw' specialists

Crystal Palace	8 (0-0s)
Everton	8
Leeds	7
Arsenal	6
Coventry	6
Liverpool	6
Newcastle	6
Norwich	6
Sheffield Wednesday	6
Aston Villa	5

(Ipswich Town were the only club who didn't have a single 0-0 draw all season)

Six teams that conceded more than one own goal

Coventry	4
Manchester City	4
QPR	4
Ipswich	3
Chelsea	2
Leicester	2

Top 10 Tattoos

Vinny Jones	(Welsh dragon over heart)
Vinny Jones	(English rose on forearm)
Eric Cantona	(Indian chief on chest)
Ian Wright	(Motorbike on leg)
John Hartson	(Welsh combo on leg)
Lee Sharpe	(Indian chief on shoulder)
Stuart Pearce	(Strange thing on arm)
Vinny Jones	('Wimbledon, Wembley 1988' on leg)
Vinny Jones	('Division Two Champions, Leeds, 1991/92' on other leg)
Vinny Jones	('Sam Forever' on left buttock, allegedly)

Top 10 'High scoring teams'

Blackburn	(scored)	80
Manchester United		77
Nottingham Forest		72
Newcastle		67
Tottenham		66
Liverpool		65
QPR		61
Southampton		61
Leeds		59
Manchester City		53

Top 10 Clubs with the most away wins

Blackburn	10
Manchester United	10
Nottingham Forest	10
Liverpool	8
Leeds	7
Arsenal	7
Newcastle	6
Tottenham	6
Chelsea	6
Sheffield Wednesday	6

Top 10 Haircuts

Barry Venison	(Highlights on *Match of the Day*)
Stan Collymore	(Blonde version)
David James	(Collymore copycat)
Darren Peacock	(Why?)
Ray Parlour	(Worzel love-child)
Graham Le Saux	(Fluffty tufty)
Warren Barton	(Blondes have more fun)
David Seaman	(Mmmm interesting, not)
Jason Lee	(Defender distractor)
Steve McManaman	(Curly wurly)

Stats

Ten teams who kept scoring in the 90th minute

Southampton	6 times
Aston Villa	4
Leicester	4
Leeds	4
Liverpool	4
Manchester Utd	4
Arsenal	2
QPR	2
Sheffield Wednesday	2
Wimbledon	2

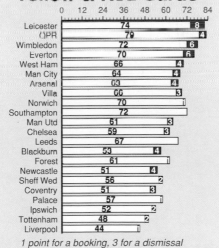

Yellow & Red Cards

0 12 24 36 48 60 72 84

	Yellow	Red
Leicester	74	8
QPR	79	4
Wimbledon	72	6
Everton	70	6
West Ham	66	4
Man City	64	4
Arsenal	63	4
Villa	66	3
Norwich	70	
Southampton	72	
Man Utd	61	3
Chelsea	59	3
Leeds	67	
Blackburn	53	4
Forest	61	
Newcastle	51	4
Sheff Wed	56	2
Coventry	51	3
Palace	57	
Ipswich	52	2
Tottenham	48	2
Liverpool	44	1

1 point for a booking, 3 for a dismissal

Ten great Premiership hat-tricks

Ndlovu (Coventry)	v	Liverpool	March 14th	(Anfield)
Kanchelskis (Man Utd)	v	Man City	Nov 10th	(Old Trafford)
Shearer (Blackburn)	v	QPR	Nov 26th	(Ewood Park)
Shearer (Blackburn)	v	West Ham	Jan 2nd	(Ewood Park)
Shearer (Blackburn)	v	Ipswich	Jan 28th	(Ewood Park)
Johnson (Aston Villa)	v	Wimbledon	Feb 11th	(Villa Park)
Hartson (Arsenal)	v	Norwich	Apr 1st	(Highbury)
Sheringham (Spurs)	v	Newcastle	Dec 3rd	(White Hart Lane)
Yeboah (Leeds)	v	Ipswich	Apr 5th	(Elland Road)
Cole (Man Utd)	v	Ipswich	Apr 5th	(Old Trafford)

Five players sent off twice

Ferguson (Everton)	v	Arsenal	Jan 14th	(Highbury)
	v	Leicester	Mar 4th	(Filbert Street)
Jones (Wimbledon)	v	Leicester	Sept 10th	(Selhurst Park)
	v	Newcastle	Nov 19th	(Selhurst Park)
Srnicek (Newcastle)	v	Leicester	Aug 21st	(Filbert Street)
	v	Tottenham	May 3rd	(St James' Park)
Townsend (Aston Villa)	v	Wimbledon	Nov 9th	(Selhurst Park)
	v	Arsenal	Dec 29th	(Highbury)
Wilcox (Blackburn)	v	Arsenal	Aug 31st	(Highbury)
	v	Forest	Oct 29th	(City Ground)

Five goals scored in the first minute

Chris Sutton (Blackburn) v Everton (A)
John Spencer (Chelsea) v Leicester (H)
Stuart Pearce (Forest) v Norwich (H)
Own Goal (Southampton) v Palace (H)
Andy Clarke (Wimbledon) v Newcastle (H)

Five seriously big wins

Sheffield Wed	1	Nottingham Forest	7
Aston Villa	7	Wimbledon	1
Crystal Palace	1	Liverpool	6
Manchester Utd	5	Manchester City	0
Manchester Utd	9	Ipswich	0

Top 10 Clubs with the most home wins

Blackburn	17
Manchester United	16
Newcastle	14
Liverpool	13
Leeds	13
Nottingham Forest	12
QPR	10
Tottenham	10
Wimbledon	9
West Ham	9

Top 10 'Jackpot draw' specialists

Aston Villa	7 (1-1s)
Chelsea	7
Southampton	7
Tottenham	7
Sheffield Wednesday	6
Arsenal	5
Blackburn	5
Leeds	5
Leicester	5
Liverpool	5

Top 10 penalty scorers

Shearer (Blackburn)	10
Pearce (Nottingham Forest)	4
Cantona (Manchester Utd)	4
Le Tissier (Southampton)	4
Ndlovu (Coventry)	3
Wark (Ipswich)	3
McAllister (Leeds)	3
Fowler (Liverpool)	3
Beardsley (Newcastle)	3
Dicks (West Ham)	3